The New York Times

CHANGING PERSPECTIVES

Abortion

W9-CMZ-875

EDUCATIONAL PUBLISHING
BOOKS

THE NEW YORK TIMES EDITORIAL STAFF

Published in 2019 by New York Times Educational Publishing
in association with The Rosen Publishing Group, Inc.
29 East 21st Street, New York, NY 10010

First Edition

The New York Times
Alex Ward: Editorial Director, Book Development
Phyllis Collazo: Photo Rights/Permissions Editor
Heidi Giovine: Administrative Manager

Rosen Publishing
Megan Kellerman: Managing Editor
Greg Tucker: Creative Director
Brian Garvey: Art Director

Cataloging-in-Publication Data
Names: New York Times Company.
Title: Abortion / edited by the New York Times editorial staff.
Description: New York : New York Times Educational Publishing,
2019. | Series: Changing perspectives | Includes glossary and index.
Identifiers: ISBN 9781642821437 (library bound) | ISBN
9781642821420 (pbk.) | ISBN 9781642821444 (ebook)
Subjects: LCSH: Abortion—Juvenile literature. | Abortion—Moral
and ethical aspects—Juvenile literature.
Classification: LCC HQ767.A267 2019 | DDC 179.7'6—dc23

Manufactured in the United States of America

On the cover: Pro-choice and pro-life activists demonstrate near
the Supreme Court after the March for Life in Washington, Friday,
Jan. 25, 2013, the week that marked the 40th anniversary of the
Supreme Court's landmark Roe v. Wade decision; Drew Angerer
for The New York Times.

Contents

Roe v. Wade and the Evolution of Abortion Law

CHAPTER 3

Pro-Life vs. Pro-Choice

CHAPTER 4

The Uncertain Future of U.S. Abortion Rights

Introduction

THE HISTORY OF ABORTION in the United States is complex. This is partially because it cannot be wholly known, as for the majority of American history, abortion was not only illegal, but a social and moral taboo. In the past, women sought methods to terminate unwanted pregnancy through dangerous channels, often at their own risk. They relied on whisper networks to find medical care, even if it could not be provided by a medical professional. In desperate cases, women would attempt to self-induce abortion without medical oversight of any kind, using methods they had heard about through anecdote or folklore. They ingested abortifacients — substances that induce abortion — or sought surgical procedures that were highly dangerous. It's impossible to know how many cases resulted in death or irreparable harm to women seeking abortion by any means necessary in a society hostile to abortion access.

One of the reasons abortion has proven difficult to legislate and even discuss is because motivations to seek abortion are extremely varied and divisive. In the early 20th century, reasons often cited in news coverage included fetuses that were very likely or guaranteed to be born with birth defects of some kind, whether developmental or hereditary. A doctor might determine a fetus is no longer viable, meaning that the pregnancy would not result in the birth of a liveborn baby. A woman's health, physical or psychological, would be at risk if she carried the pregnancy to term. The woman might be a victim of rape or incest, which resulted in unwanted pregnancy. The mother might already have a number of children, and she and her family would not be able to afford care for another child.

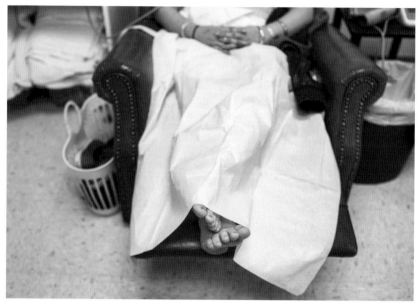

A woman waiting in the recovery area after her abortion at a clinic in Montgomery, Ala.

In the latter half of the 20th century, the Supreme Court's landmark decision in the case of Roe v. Wade emphasized a woman's legal right to privacy, which extended to her right to seek an abortion; however, individual U.S. states remain responsible for their own legislation and access to abortion, if any. Whatever a woman's reason might be to terminate a pregnancy, people have protested for or against abortion access for decades. Advocates have historically emphasized a woman's bodily autonomy and the right to choose, while those who oppose abortion cite religious, moral or ethical reasons against it.

While medical advances have made abortions safer and improved birth control methods so fewer abortions are necessary, individuals, organizations and state governments remain largely divided on the issue. Debates on when life begins, who should be involved in the decision to get an abortion and political agendas are all inextricably linked in the history of the intensely individual experience of a woman seeking to terminate a pregnancy.

CHAPTER 1

A History of Illegal Operations

In 1873, political reformer Anthony Comstock successfully lob-
bied for the enactment of the Comstock Laws, strict statutes
that prohibited the circulation of any "obscene" item related to
contraception or abortion. The Comstock Laws persisted into
the 20th century, and though many of them were declared
unconstitutional over time, anti-abortion sentiment pre-
vailed and abortions were often referred to as simply "illegal
operations" in news coverage. Medical professionals were
arrested for participating in abortion rings, and women relied
on whisper networks to find services that could be unsafe or
even life-threatening. Abortion began to enter a larger public
discussion with cases such as that of Sherri Finkbine.

Examinations in the Malpractice Cases.

BY THE NEW YORK TIMES | APRIL 24, 1873

"DR." WRIGHT, of No. 51 Bleecker-street, was before Commissioner
Osborn yesterday afternoon for examination on a charge of sending
through the mails medicines intended to be used in malpractice cases,
in violation of the recent act of Congress on that subject.

Mr. Anthony Comstock was examined on behalf of the prosecution.
He stated that he saw the advertisement of "Dr." Wright in the Her-
ald, and immediately judged of its character. He then opened a correspondence with "Dr." Wright, sending registered letters, in one of

which he inclosed $10. He received from his medical correspondent a package containing a box of pills and a paper, with directions for using the same. The letters and package were put in evidence, and the District-Attorney rested the case for the Government on Mr. Comstock's testimony.

Counsel for the defense moved for the discharge of the prisoner on the ground that no case had been made against him. The Commissioner denied the motion. Counsel then asked for an adjournment until to-day, stating that he would show that the prisoner was not the guilty party, but that he merely furnished money to an impecunious medical practitioner who carried on the business. By consent of the District-Attorney, the further hearing was postponed until to-day.

The examination of "Dr." Francis E. Andrews, of No. 360 Lexington-avenue, charged with violating the section of the Post-office law prohibiting the sending of obscene publications, &c., through the mails, was commenced yesterday before United States Commissioner Andrews. Anthony Comstock, the only witness examined, testified with reference to his correspondence with the accused. The hearing was then adjourned until Saturday.

"Dr." E. Gardner, of No. 202 Broadway, was arrested yesterday on a similar charge, and committed by Commissioner Osborn for examination in default of giving $5,000 bail.

Doctor and Nurses Held

BY THE NEW YORK TIMES | JULY 12, 1937

Raiders accuse four of performing illegal operations.

A DOCTOR, TWO NURSES and an attendant who were arrested by Brooklyn police Saturday night were arraigned in Felony Court yesterday on charges of performing illegal operations.

Magistrate Blanchfield held the doctor in $2,500 bail and the others in $1,000 bail each for further hearing on July 16. Those arraigned were: Dr. Louis Duke, 51 years old, and Charlotte Foder, 45, a nurse, both of 551 Bedford Avenue, Brooklyn; Mary Corrigan, 29, of 54 West 186th Street, the Bronx, also a nurse, and Olive Leonard, 40, of 181 Lenox Road, Brooklyn.

The police said raiders found four women patients in the doctor's office at the Bedford Avenue address.

Woman Juror Fails to End a Deadlock

BY THE NEW YORK TIMES | OCT. 7, 1937

Foreman tries in vain to win four over for conviction in abortion case.

AFTER HAVING THE evidence under heated discussion for exactly six hours, a General Sessions jury, with the foreman the only woman member, reported just before 6 o'clock last night inability to agree on a verdict in the abortion trial of Mrs. Emily F. Kane, 65 years old, of 233 Bleecker Street.

Judge Owen W. Bohan discharged the jury and again released the defendant in the $1,000 bail she posted on her indictment last January. Assistant District Attorney Martin Binder did not indicate whether he would call Mrs. Kane for trial again.

The jurors stood eight to four for conviction, with the foreman, Mrs. Rose Cooper, a young housewife of 178 Norfolk Street, voting "guilty" on each ballot. It was said she was reluctant to send word to the judge that they could not agree. She was the first woman to be chosen as jury foreman in the history of General Sessions.

"I have learned a lot since I was selected to serve as a juror in this case," Mrs. Cooper remarked as she and the other jurors were filing out of the court. Judge Bohan, after discharging them, told the jurors that in the last eighteen years Mrs. Kane had been arrested on five abortion charges. He added that, except the one on which she was tried, each time she was discharged in a Magistrate's Court.

Mrs. Cooper was calm as the jurors filed into the box to be discharged. Several of the men were openly hostile to those who had not joined them and their foreman on a verdict. It was reported that Mrs. Cooper took the leading part in the efforts of the majority to induce the minority, particularly one juror who declared he would "stick for acquittal till hell freezes over," to vote with them, recalling in detail the prosecution's evidence against the elderly defendant.

Five women and seven men who comprised the jury in the trial of Morris Unger, a chemist, on a larceny indictment, missed the opportunity of deliberating on a verdict when Judge James G. Wallace, in another part of the court, directed them at the close of testimony to acquit the defendant. Unger was discharged.

Illegal Operations Laid to 3 Doctors

BY THE NEW YORK TIMES | NOV. 16, 1940

Two other men seized as members of the alleged ring.

FIVE MEN, THREE of whom were physicians, were arrested yesterday as suspects in an investigation into an abortion ring that had been operating in this city for a year. The ring was said by Assistant District Attorney Aaron Benenson, who is in charge of the inquiry, to have distributed circulars and cards to drug stores advertising its activities.

The suspects are Dr. Louis G. Small, 38 years old, of 36-06 Thirtieth Street, Long Island City, who was arrested in a five-story building at 65 East Eightieth Street known as the Security Health Foundation, Inc.; Dr. William Lenetska, 51, of 215 West Eight-third Street, who has an office at 1749 Grand Concourse, the Bronx; Dr. Pierron Bergen, 49, of 32-16 Forty-fifth Street, Astoria, alleged to be an associate of Dr. Small at the East Eightieth Street address; Mack Goodman, 56, of 222 Bedford Park Boulevard, the Bronx, and Harry P. Flum, 60, of 401 West Forty-sixth Street.

Dr. Small was released in $5,000 bail and the others in $1,000 each in Felony Court for a hearing Dec. 3. They pleaded not guilty. Dr. Lenetska was taken into custody as he left a house at an undisclosed address on the West Side where, it was charged, he had just performed an illegal operation at which Dr. Small was present. Dr. Bergen was arrested as he was discharged from the Bellevue Hospital psychiatric ward, where he had been a patient for acute alcoholism, the prosecutor said.

Suggests Doctors Relax 'Hypocrisy'

BY THE NEW YORK TIMES | JAN. 31, 1942

CHARGING THE MEDICAL profession with "hypocrisy" in its attitude toward therapeutic abortion, Dr. Alan F. Guttmacher, Associate professor of Obstetrics in the Johns Hopkins University School of Medicine, suggested yesterday that the profession relax its barriers and thus "cheat the criminal abortionist."

Dr. Guttmacher, who spoke at the closing session of the three-day annual meeting of the Birth Control Federation of America in the Hotel Waldorf-Astoria, made clear that he was referring only to therapeutic abortion in cases where pregnancy might endanger the health or threaten the life of the mother.

He cited the estimate of Special Prosecutor John Harlon Amen that there were from 100,000 to 250,000 criminal abortions performed each year in New York City and saw the feeling of the medical profession as a major cause of these operations.

"Wouldn't we be better off if we relaxed some of our indications for therapeutic abortion and thus cheated the criminal abortionist?" Dr. Guttmacher asked. "And, furthermore, it is generally demonstrated that up to 85 per cent of the women involved are married women. Three per cent are widowed and 12 per cent single women. The patient hypocrisy and holier-than-thou attitude of the medical profession in regard to this problem is revolting."

As ailments "making pregnancy ill-advised," Dr. Guttmacher listed four diseases and added a fifth by remarking that "in the dictator nations the glories of extravagant fecundity are extolled as a virtue far in excess of godliness or goodness."

Dr. Guttmacher pointed out "heredity blemishes on family trees which make it safer not to garner the fruit, or perhaps at the most just an apple or two, as medical indications for contraception or sterilization. He listed epilepsy, congenital deafness due to morbid heredity, feeble-mindedness and other inherited conditions.

A report of the federation's medical department showed increasing support from public health departments and health officers in the birth control movement. It pointed to 209 city and county health departments giving birth control service and another 198 referring cases to private physicians and clinics.

Ninety per cent of health officers replying to a questionnaire, according to the report, stated they were in favor of using some part of Federal maternal and child health funds for birth control service.

"We feel," the report added, "that these reports are significant as an indication of broad acceptance of the necessity of family planning and that they merit follow-up."

Inclusion of contraceptive service in existing programs was discussed by Mrs. William R. Talbot, R. N., superintendent of the Babies Hospital in Philadelphia. Mrs. Stuart Mudd, director of the Marriage Counsel, Philadelphia, spoke of the clinic patient, with emphasis on the problems of emotional maladjustments.

Legal Abortions Proposed in Code

BY ANTHONY LEWIS | MAY 22, 1959

Law Institute draft restricts use and curbs imposition of the death penalty.

WASHINGTON, MAY 21 — The American Law Institute approved today a proposal to permit legal therapeutic abortions, under controlled conditions, for the sake of the mother or the unborn child.

The provision is part of the model penal code being drafted by the institute, an organization of judges, lawyers and law teachers dedicated to studies of the law. Institute proposals are frequently reflected in state statutes and judicial decisions.

The section approved today would permit a doctor to perform an abortion under any of these circumstances:

• If continuation of the pregnancy "would gravely impair the physical or mental health of the mother."

• If the doctor believes "the child would be born with grave physical or mental defect."

• If the pregnancy resulted from rape or incest.

A further requirement was that two physicians certify in writing their belief that one of these circumstances existed before the abortion was performed.

There was some opposition to the abortion proposal on the floor of the Law Institute meeting. But an effort to delete the provision for legalization was beaten by an overwhelming voice vote.

DEATH PENALTY REVIEWED

The institute also approved a new procedure for determining when the death sentence shall be imposed in murder cases.

This section provides, first, that the judge alone may impose a non-capital sentence if certain mitigating circumstances exist. Among these are a guilty plea by the defendant, his youth, doubts about the verdict of guilty, lack of a prior criminal history and existence of mental or emotional disturbance at the time of the crime.

Second, if the judge does not decide upon a non-capital sentence at the end of the trial, the model code provision calls for a further proceeding on what the sentence should be. At this proceeding evidence would be produced of the prisoner's character and background.

The draft offered alternative sections permitting either the judge or the jury to fix the sentence after this further proceeding. The members voted today, 78 to 35, to express a preference for jury determination.

The significance of the sentencing proposal is that it gets away from the prevailing state practice of giving juries absolute power to fix the death penalty.

STATE LAW ON ABORTION

New York State law, like that of many states, provides that abortion is lawful if it is "necessary to preserve the life of the woman or of the child with which she is pregnant."

Several states further require that at least two physicians certify in writing that the termination of pregnancy is "essential" for medical reasons. New York State does not spell out the necessity of such certification, but hospitals and medical societies have filled the gap with strict requirements on the matter.

In some cases, as many as five physicians must certify that the termination is therapeutic.

Dilemma Is Seen in Abortion Law

BY THE NEW YORK TIMES | JULY 28, 1959

MORE THAN 90 PER CENT of the therapeutic abortions performed at Mount Sinai Hospital during the last six years were illegal by the strict interpretation of the law, according to the hospital's director of obstetrics and gynecology.

Dr. Alan F. Guttmacher, the obstetrician, in a magazine article, said that a hospital using the liberal interpretation that Mount Sinai did "literally places itself and its doctors in jeopardy of prosecution for illegal abortion many times during the course of a year."

The article appears in the August issue of Redbook magazine.

Dr. Guttmacher said yesterday in an interview that a majority of the therapeutic abortions performed in hospitals throughout the United States, except Roman Catholic hospitals, were illegal.

HIS VIEW IS BACKED

His view was supported by Dr. Glenn Craig of San Francisco, head of the American College of Obstetrics and Gynecology, who said in a telephone interview that the "illegal" abortions were "morally and medically correct."

Dr. Guttmacher wrote that in most states, abortion was legal only when necessary to save the life of the mother, but that a few states had broadened the law to include preservation of the mother's "health" or "safety" or the prevention of "serious or permanent bodily injury to her."

Dr. Craig said, "One of our big problems is that the abortion law like all laws concerning medicine is very specific. It is impossible to change the law. It must be left up to the enforcement officers. Our responsibility is for the health and welfare of our patients."

He said that he had been told that "an honest doctor with a clean record" had never been arrested for performing such abortions as Dr. Guttmacher cited.

Dr. Guttmacher wrote that at Mount Sinai, from 1953 to 1958, there had been 147 therapeutic abortions. "Altogether abortion preserved the lives of perhaps a dozen of these 147 women," he wrote.

"In the rest we believe it contributed significantly to the preservation of physical, emotional or mental health, though the law does not recognize these as proper reasons for abortion," he went on. "By the strictest interpretation of the law, then, more than 90 per cent of these abortions were illegal."

Of the 147 abortions, he said, 39 per cent were performed for psychiatric reasons, 31 per cent to prevent the birth of abnormal children, 10 per cent because of past or present cancer in the mother and 10 per cent because of other physical problems.

Abortion Suit Is Filed

SPECIAL TO THE NEW YORK TIMES | JULY 26, 1962

PHOENIX, ARIZ., JULY 25 — A young Phoenix mother who fears that she is going to have a deformed baby because she took a drug filed suit today for a declaratory judgment against the legality of Arizona's law forbidding abortion.

Mrs. Sherri Finkbine, mother of four children, took the action after telling psychiatrists earlier today that "it would upset me terribly to have a deformed baby." She is three months pregnant.

The 29-year-old matron, also a Phoenix television personality, feared her children would be permanently affected by the drug Thalidomide. The drug was contained in a dozen or more tranquilizers she took recently.

She was joined in the suit by Steven Morris, administrative officer of Good Samaritan Hospital. Mr. Morris said the hospital would furnish its services for an abortion once court approval was granted.

The suit was filed in Superior Court late today. Charles N. Romano, Maricopa County attorney, said he would reply to the suit immediately and press for an early determination.

The abortion, which had been scheduled for tomorrow, was halted after a meeting of the medical staff and legal counsel of the hospital.

Two psychiatrists apparently found that Mrs. Finkbine's mental health would be affected if she continued to carry the baby.

The drug has been blamed for more than 5,000 abnormal births in West Germany, England, Canada and Australia. It has been banned in this country. The woman, however, took it in sleeping pills her husband bought in England last year.

Abortion is illegal in Arizona unless the mother's life is clearly in danger.

Sherri Finkbine with three of her children.

Officials of the hospital and the Maricopa County Medical Society said no decision was likely for several days.

According to published medical reports, the drug causes phocomelia. This is a type of atrophy in which babies are born without arms or legs, or with only small stumps.

Phoenix Abortion Ruling Delayed

SPECIAL TO THE NEW YORK TIMES | JULY 28, 1962

PHOENIX, ARIZ., JULY 27 — A Superior Court judge postponed today a decision on whether an expectant mother who took the drug Thalidomide should be allowed to have a legal abortion.

Judge Yale said he would rule Monday on a motion to dismiss the case. He said he was ready to start trial immediately, if he decided that Mrs. Sherri Finkbine's suit was in order.

Mrs. Finkbine, 30 years old and the mother of four children, and her husband, Robert, were joined by the Good Samaritan Hospital in asking the court to allow the abortion, which is forbidden by Arizona law unless the health of the mother is clearly in danger.

Felix Gordon, deputy Maricopa County Attorney, moved for dismissal of the case on technical grounds that no controversy existed.

Walter Cheifetz, a lawyer representing the Finkbines, said a quick decision was necessary. He quoted physicians as saying Mrs. Finkbine either must have a therapeutic abortion within two weeks or undergo abdominal surgery.

Mrs. Finkbine
Undergoes Abortion in Sweden

SPECIAL TO THE NEW YORK TIMES | AUG. 19, 1962

Surgeon asserts unborn child was deformed — mother of four took thalidomide.

STOCKHOLM, SWEDEN, AUG. 18 — Mrs. Robert Finkbine of Phoenix, Ariz., who received permission here yesterday for a legal abortion, was operated upon successfully this morning.

The 30-year-old mother of four healthy children was informed after the operation that the fetus was deformed, as she had feared.

Her fears arose four weeks ago when she learned that she had inadvertently taken the drug thalidomide, which is blamed for the birth of thousands of deformed infants in Europe and Canada.

The abortion panel of the Royal Swedish Medical Board granted Mrs. Finkbine's request for today's operation to safeguard her "mental health."

"We felt we were doing the right thing all along for Sherri's mental health," her husband told reporters in a hospital corridor.

"Now we know we were right for the baby as well. The last thing we wanted to do was to bring a deformed youngster into the world if it could be prevented," Mr. Finkbine said.

The couple had made several unsuccessful attempts to obtain a legal abortion in Arizona, where the law allows such operations only if the expectant mother's life is in peril. They flew here Aug. 5 because of Sweden's more liberal abortion law.

Mr. Finkbine said his wife entered the Royal Caroline Hospital at 7 p. m. yesterday. The operation was begun at 8:30 o'clock this morning. It lasted about forty-five minutes.

Mr. Finkbine said that he and his wife had been told that the operation was "a complete success" and that there were no complications. Mrs. Finkbine was in about the thirteenth week of her pregnancy.

It is expected that Mrs. Finkbine will remain in the hospital for six to eight days. She and her husband will probably leave Sweden a day or two later.

He said that he had to get back home by the end of this month for the football practice that will begin at the high school where he teaches history. Mr. Finkbine, who is 31, is a line coach.

He estimated that the expenses of the trip to Sweden would amount to $4,000. He said that he expected to meet them through a first-person story of the case that has been sold to several European newspapers.

"I don't particularly like doing this," he said, "but it is better than trying to pay debts for several years on a high school teacher's salary."

The Finkbine Case had its beginning in London last year. Chaperoning sixty-four high school students on a European tour, Mr. Finkbine obtained some thalidomide and carried the leftover pills home.

Mrs. Finkbine, a hostess on a television program for children, took thirty-six of the sedative pills in the early stages of her pregnancy. Neither she nor her husband was aware until four weeks ago that the pills contained thalidomide.

Abortion: Once a Whispered Problem, Now a Public Debate

BY JANE E. BRODY | JAN. 8, 1968

IN 1962, THE local veterans' organizations in Rapid City, S. D., named LaVange Michael, a widow then 68 years old, as its "Gold Star Mother of the Year."

Three weeks after receiving this honor, Mrs. Michael was arrested for performing an abortion on a Minneapolis secretary who nearly died as a result of the septic operation.

By her own admission to this reporter, the elderly widow — a one-time nurses' aide — had been doing abortions since 1932 at prices ranging from $25 to whatever the traffic would bear. Her clients — eight or nine a week — came from all over the country. She assured herself of future business by giving each customer a small, white calling card.

When Mrs. Michael pleaded guilty to the abortion charge, the county attorney breathed a sigh of relief. He had wondered how he would be able to select a jury that he could be sure had in no way been helped by the defendant.

Mrs. Michael counts among her friends some of Rapid City's most prestigious citizens. Her son is a highly respected optometrist in the city of 43,000 and her daughter is married to a city councilman.

In a recent conversation, Sheriff Glenn Best asserted that until the Minneapolis girl had signed a complaint, he was unable to build a good case against Mrs. Michael, although virtually the entire town knew what went on in her attractive bungalow just a few blocks from the county courthouse.

Even the local medical society was not particularly anxious to put an end to Mrs. Michael's career, Sheriff Best said.

The widow finished serving her sentence — three years' probation — last June.

HER CASE TYPIFIES PROBLEM

The case of the Rapid City Gold Star Mother typifies the abortion scene that has existed in cities and towns throughout the country for many years. Although abortion as a word was whispered behind closed doors, abortion as a practice has long been tolerated more or less as a necessary evil, something — as one Rapid City woman put it — "we swept under the rug."

In the last few years, however, interested men and women in many states have been peeking under the edge of the rug to see what is there and what might be done about it.

A four-week study of the current abortion picture indicates that their curiosity already has spurred several major changes:

• It has brought abortion into public debate and cocktail party conversation thereby helping to dispel many myths long associated with both legal and illegal abortions.

• It has compelled many persons who are seeking a liberalization of abortion laws — clergymen, doctors and others — to risk their reputations and often their jobs by helping women with unwanted pregnancies.

• It has spurred many persons previously opposed to abortion law reform — including a number of prominent Roman Catholics — to restudy the matter and come out in favor of a change in the laws.

• And it has succeeded in liberalizing the abortion laws in three states — Colorado, California and North Carolina — with many more states expected soon to follow suit.

"It is really remarkable how much the climate of public opinion has changed in just a few years," observed Robert W. McCoy, coordinator of the Minnesota Council for the Legal Termination of Pregnancy.

"I wouldn't be surprised if several states including Minnesota soon repealed their abortion laws and left the matter to physicians and their patients."

Until Colorado changed its law last April, abortion was a crime in all 50 states except to save the life of the mother. The District of Columbia and five of the states, including Colorado, permitted abortion when the mother's health was endangered by the pregnancy. The other states were Alabama, Maryland, Oregon and New Mexico.

DOCTORS STRETCH THE LAW

In actual practice, however, many doctors throughout the nation have been stretching, twisting and torturing the law to fit what they regard as real medical needs — such as abortion when the mental as well as the physical health of the mother was threatened, or when her child was likely to be born seriously malformed.

These "extralegal" abortions have usually been justified on the grounds that carrying the pregnancy to term would so damage the woman's mental health that she might attempt suicide.

But extralegal hospital abortions have been an almost exclusive privilege of well-to-do women — particularly those who know about and can afford the psychiatric consultation recommending abortion to avert a possible suicide.

To Dr. Robert Hall, an obstetrician at Columbia-Presbyterian Medical Center and associate professor of obstetrics at Columbia University's College of Physicians and Surgeons, stringent abortion laws have forced both women and their doctors into a highly hypocritical situation. In a typical year, he said, 80 per cent of an estimated 800 hospital abortions in New York City are performed for "psychiatric reasons" to avert suicide.

"Yet, we know that all these women are not suicidal," the doctor said. "The abortions are done to preserve maternal health, not life."

"Abortion reform would permit us legally to do the hospital abortions that the more courageous obstetricians are now doing," Dr. Hall explained. "About 90 per cent of obstetricians simply tell their patients, 'I cannot help you,' period."

Even the woman of means must go through a tricky and elaborate procedure to obtain a hospital abortion. She must find the right doctor, the right psychiatrist, the right hospital with the right abortion committee.

The head of the abortion committee at one Middle Western hospital said that the decisions of these committees were often arbitrary. Some committee members may be swayed by animosity toward certain referring physicians or by the decisions of other members of the committee. In any case, he said, it is the patient who gets shortchanged.

The woman without means or appropriate connections often finds herself seeking an end to her unwanted pregnancy in a bleak, dirty underworld where the Mrs. Michaels and many less savory characters thrive.

ESTIMATES MAY BE EXAGGERATED

There are no reliable statistics on what goes on in this underworld. Estimates place the number of criminal abortions in this country each year at from 200,000 to one million. But the often quoted estimate that these clandestine dealings result in the death of 8,000 to 10,000 women each year has been called highly exaggerated. Dr. Christopher Tietze of the Population Council says the number of deaths is more likely 500 or, at most, 1,000.

However, the victims of criminal abortions pay a heavy toll in terms of permanent injury and sterility.

For example, at Lincoln Hospital, in a socioeconomically deprived area of the Bronx, doctors finish about 400 abortions a year that have been botched up by amateurs. Dr. J. J. Smith, head of the hospital's obstetrics department, said that "at least 20 per cent of these women are admitted to the hospital seriously ill."

"Many suffer permanent kidney damage and sterility," he said. "Last year one girl died of a tetanus infection."

Most of the hospital's abortion victims are women with several children at home who felt that they simply could not house or feed another child.

Similar problems arise for the middle-class young woman who finds herself pregnant out of wedlock. Joan R., a 21-year-old New York girl who has been struggling along as a theatrical technician, said that in her job, "I could not even afford to be pregnant, much less have a baby."

Joan was unable to turn to her parents for help, and the abortion she obtained from a careless Pennsylvania doctor left her sterile for life.

The Rev. Howard R. Moody, pastor of Judson Memorial Church in Greenwich Village, is one of 31 New York City clergymen who are trying to help women like Joan take care of their problem pregnancies with a minimum of risk to their life and health.

The clergymen, Protestant and Jewish, formed a consultation service last June "to offer advice and counsel" to those women who are being "driven into the underworld of criminality or the dangerous practice of self-induced abortion."

NEW YORK POST ARCHIVES/GETTY IMAGES

The Rev. Howard R. Moody in June 1959. The Reverend is an outspoken advocate of reform.

CLERGYMEN COUNSELED 800 WOMEN

A woman seeking the service's aid calls 477-0034 and obtains through a recording the names and numbers of participating clergymen in various parts of the city. Then she must make an appointment with the clergyman of her choice.

In the service's first five months, the clergymen counseled well over 800 women — half of them married, 20 per cent of them Negro and more than half of them between the ages of 18 and 25.

In all cases, the service provided "the best medical advice to take care of the problem pregnancy," Mr. Moody said. He added that about 90 per cent of the women chose to go through with an abortion.

Mr. Moody expects that clergymen in other cities will soon be offering similar services to women with problem pregnancies.

Such help also is being offered by a number of persons active in efforts to liberalize abortion laws. One of them, Lawrence Lader, has told college forums at Cornell University, Harvard Medical School and Michigan State University that he will get "the best medical services" for "any woman in need."

Mr. Lader said that since his book, "Abortion," was published in April, 1966, by Bobbs-Merrill ($5.95), he has helped 400 women who have called or written to him.

Mr. Lader and others like him who are openly defying abortion laws believe they are acting in good faith to meet a "human need" that is not being answered by "cruel, inhuman laws."

PUBLICITY CAUSED A CHANGE

Efforts to reform these laws received their initial impetus in 1962 when Mrs. Robert (Sherri) Finkbine, a Phoenix, Ariz., mother of four, inadvertently took the birth-deforming drug thalidomide during the early weeks of her fifth pregnancy.

The fate of Mrs. Finkbine showed that stretching of abortion laws was not enough. Doctors saw just how restricted they could be in trying to exercise their best medical judgment. Mrs. Finkbine's abortion, which at first had been approved, was denied when news accounts of her case brought it to the attention of the county attorney. He said that he would be forced to prosecute if a complaint was filed about the operation.

After much delay, Mrs. Finkbine had an abortion performed in Sweden, where doctors confirmed that her child would have been severely deformed.

The Finkbine case coincided with another development that inspired extensive discussion of the nation's abortion laws. The American Law Institute, one of the most prestigious of legal bodies, formulated a Model Penal Code to serve as a blueprint for reform of outdated criminal laws.

The code suggests a law that would permit abortions to be performed in hospitals when the patient's physician and a hospital abortion committee agree that the pregnancy is endangering the mental or physical health of the mother, or when the pregnancy resulted from rape or incest, or was likely to result in the birth of a child with serious mental or physical defects.

As rational and conservative an approach as this bill seemed to many to be, it was soon discovered that it would be anything but easy to get state legislatures to adopt it.

Even the nationwide epidemic of German measles in 1963–64 — which left in its wake 20,000 stillborn and 30,000 defective babies because their mothers had contracted the disease early in pregnancy — moved only a few legislators.

BILL LACKED DOCTORS' SUPPORT

Oddly enough, in many states it was lack of support by the doctors themselves that led to the bill's demise. In others, strong opposition from some church groups — primarily the Roman Catholic Church — made legislators fear that a vote for abortion reform would be political suicide.

The Roman Catholic Church officially takes the position that human life and the human soul begin at the moment of conception, and strictly forbids destruction of the resulting embryo. Several studies have shown, however, that Catholic women obtain abortions nearly as often as women of other faiths.

Cries of "Murder" and "Infanticide," warnings of "Fetuses first, blue-eyed Irishmen next," and displays of preserved and bottled human fetuses characterized much of the opposition that helped to kill abortion bills the first and sometimes the second time they were introduced.

But those who have been studying the situation closely are confident that at their next introduction, abortion bills will pass in many states.

Assemblyman Albert H. Blumenthal, a Manhattan Democrat who recently reintroduced his abortion reform bill into the New York State Legislature, said, "Its prospects are much improved."

He noted that, among other encouraging signs, many legislators had polled their constituents and found that the majority of voters — regardless of religion — were in favor of reforming the state's law, which permits abortion only to save the mother's life.

The legislators' findings are consistent with those of a national survey taken by the National Opinion Research Center in 1965.

Questions asked of a representative sample of 1,484 adult Americans revealed that 71 per cent would favor abortion if the woman's health was seriously endangered by the pregnancy, 56 per cent if she became pregnant as a result of rape, and 55 per cent if her child was likely to be born defective.

But when it came to social indications for abortion, 77 per cent said no to abortion if the family could not afford more children, 80 per cent said no if the woman was unmarried and did not want to marry the child's father, and 83 per cent said no if the woman was married but did not want any more children.

IN FAVOR OF LIBERALIZATION

"One of the most striking findings of the analysis," according to Alice S. Rossi, a research associate in human development at the University of Chicago, "is the relatively slight difference between Protestants and Catholics in their views on abortions."

Seventy-three per cent of the Protestants and 64 per cent of the Catholics said that they were in favor of abortion to preserve the mother's health. For rape, the figures were 57 per cent and 47 per cent respectively, and for a deformed fetus, 57 per cent and 48 per cent respectively.

While this survey is comparatively recent, many observers believe that the climate of public opinion is changing so fast that a survey today would show considerably higher percentages favoring the provisions of the model abortion law.

Some observers, among them Mr. McCoy of the Minnesota reform movement, think that a majority of adults would now sanction social indications for abortion as well. This would make abortion essentially a matter of personal choice.

Despite a history of inaction in this area, doctors also favor abortion reform, according to the results of a poll of the nation's practicing physicians taken early last year by the journal Modern Medicine.

Of 40,089 doctors who returned the questionnaire, 86.9 per cent said they were in favor of liberalizing abortion laws. Obstetricians and gynecologists were least in favor of liberalization with only 83.7 per cent voting for change as compared with 94.6 per cent of psychiatrists.

Slightly less than half the doctors who identified themselves as Roman Catholics were in favor of more liberal laws.

Well over half the physicians who answered the questionnaire said that abortion should be legally indicated in cases of risk to the mother's physical and mental health, chance of fetal deformity and pregnancy through rape or incest.

Two months after the results of the Modern Medicine poll were made public, the American Medical Association loosened its 94-year-old policy on abortion to favor the model abortion law. The association said the policy change was "in keeping with modern scientific safeguards, and permits the physician to exercises his personal conscience and medical judgment in the best interest of his patient."

This action by the largest and most powerful medical organization in the country — an organization noted for its conservatism — is expected to speed the trend toward more liberal abortion laws.

Even without a change in the laws, the new A.M.A. policy may allow doctors in at least one state to follow its recommendations. New Jersey law forbids abortions performed "without lawful justification."

In a recent statement, the state's county prosecutors interpreted this to mean that abortions could be performed in accordance with "accepted medical standards." This, in turn, could be interpreted as in accordance with A.M.A policy.

Bills to liberalize statutes on abortion were introduced during the last legislative sessions of more than 20 states. Legislators in those states where the measures were defeated are keeping a close watch on what is happening in Colorado, California and North Carolina, the three states that have enacted abortion reform legislation.

When Colorado passed its reform bill, which follows the guidelines of the Model Penal Code, opponents of reform predicted sourly that the state would become the "abortion mecca" of the nation.

EMOTIONAL REASONS CONSIDERED

This, in fact, has not happened. As Dr. David Cowen, manager of health and hospitals for the city and the county of Denver, pointed out in a recent interview:

> In the first seven months under the new law, 115 abortions were performed in Colorado, 29 of them on women from out of state. That's hardly what I'd call an 'abortion mecca'.

Dr. Cowen explained, however, that only two hospitals in the state were accepting nonresidents for therapeutic abortions. He noted that before the law was two months old, the Colorado Medical Society strongly recommended that the statute should be limited to state residents.

"However, illness, including illness in pregnancy, does not respect state lines," Dr. Cowen commented. "If a heart patient who happens to live in Nevada can best be treated in Denver, we accept him. Why should we turn our backs on a nonresident who has a legitimate need for an abortion that can best be handled here?"

Most of the abortions done under the new Colorado law have been to preserve the mental health of the mother. This is the provision of abortion reform laws that has most frightened their opponents, who predict that it will lead to abortion on demand.

Dr. Abraham Heller, a Denver psychiatrist who has counseled many of the women treated under the new law, said:

> We are being very, very careful and discriminating. After all, there are few guidelines on what may be the proper psychiatric indications for abortion.
>
> Some women who have come to us for abortions have gotten pregnant for important emotional reasons they're not even aware of. To grant them the abortion might do more harm than good.

In at least one Colorado hospital — Denver General — abortions that are medically indicated are done without regard to the patients' marital status. As Dr. Cowen said, "If a woman will suffer damage to her mental or physical health, it is just as real whether she is married or not."

MORE RESTRICTIVE LAWS

California and North Carolina enacted somewhat less liberal abortion laws than Colorado. The California statute does not allow abortion when the child is likely to be deformed, and North Carolina excludes nonresidents from the benefits of its law.

Many reformers are now willing to admit that the model abortion law would barely touch the huge iceberg of criminal abortion. Mr. Moody noted that 99 per cent of the women his service has helped would not qualify for a hospital abortion even under the reform bill.

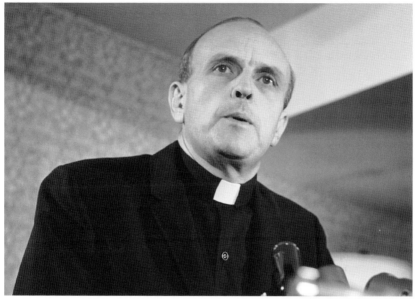

The Rev. Robert F. Drinan proposed a repeal of all laws against abortion in the first six months of pregnancy. He made the proposal in a speech before the International Conference on Abortion in Washington, Sept. 7, 1967.

"The main reasons these women sought an abortion were emotional or economic," he said.

The Illinois Citizens for the Medical Control of Abortion advocates repeal of all laws governing abortions performed by licensed physicians. The reform group in Minnesota expects that a repeal bill will be introduced in the next legislative session, and that it may even have the backing of the state medical society.

Perhaps the most surprising move in the direction of repeal was made this fall by the Rev. Robert F. Drinan, a Roman Catholic priest and dean of the Boston College Law School. At an international abortion conference sponsored by the Kennedy Foundation and the Harvard Divinity School, Father Drinan described repeal as a more legally acceptable position than reform.

He said that he was strongly opposed to putting the state in the position of "deciding who shall live and who shall die," as he said would be the case under the reform bill.

"It's a terrible thing to say in the law that we don't want any deformed or retarded children around," he said in an interview. "Furthermore, I think that the 'mental and physical health of the mother' is as phony as a $3 bill."

Father Drinan added that the model abortion law "won't reach the real problem, namely that 80 to 85 per cent of the abortions are for married women who just don't want this third, fourth or fifth child."

"This is a social problem, not a medical one," he asserted.

His conclusion:

If you say a problem exists, and that women will get an abortion and the law can't prevent this, all right then, withdraw the law. If we're going to have to change, I say the nonlaw has greater potential for solving the problem than the Model Penal Code.

Father Drinan and others pointed out that in a few years medical science will have made all abortion laws obsolete. Already under study are two kinds of drugs that can abort a woman in the very early stages of pregnancy.

One drug, referred to as the "morning-after" pill, can be taken up to six days after a woman has sexual intercourse, at a time when she is likely to be fertile. If she has conceived, the drug blocks implantation of the fertilized egg.

The other drug, called the Swedish "M-pill," initiates menstrual flow when taken once a month at the end of the menstrual cycle — regardless of whether or not the woman has conceived.

In both cases, the woman never knows if she really was pregnant. If not, well and good. If so, she has an instant, safe and sure abortion in the privacy of her personal life.

Again the Abortion Issue

BY JAMES F. CLARITY | JAN. 14, 1968

ALBANY — When Governor Rockefeller unexpectedly called last week for a liberalization of the state's 85-year-old abortion law, he raised the cautious hopes of the minority of legislators who favor reform of the law and stirred the embers of what was one of the blazing issues of the 1967 session.

Loaded with emotional opinions bred in conflicting religious and humanistic beliefs, the abortion issue set Democrat against Democrat, Republican against Republican and Catholic against non-Catholic in the legislative chambers last year. The result was the death of a bill that would have broadened the grounds for legal abortion, which is now permitted only to save a mother's life.

The 1967 abortion measure would have legalized abortions when there was substantial risk of impaired mental or physical health if pregnancy were to continue, when the infant would be born defective, or when the pregnancy resulted from incest or rape.

Governor Rockefeller, who stayed largely apart from last year's legislative struggle, did not endorse those specific proposals last week, but he did see a need to "try to find a basis for reconciling the different points of view which will permit us to catch up with many other areas. ... There is a great deal of human tragedy involved here and I think a lot could be done to alleviate it."

REPORT EXPECTED

In the light of that statement, his earlier promise to appoint a committee to recommend reform of the law took on new significance. The committee is expected to make its recommendations at the current session, and the general presumption in the Capitol is that the Governor would sign a revised law if it was approved by the Legislature.

There was no presumption, however, that reform will come at the current session. Although a reliable public opinion survey published last week showed that 98 per cent of the Jews, 83 per cent of the Protestants and 72 per cent of the Catholics polled favored revision of the law, opposition to such revision is still formidable in both the Senate and the Assembly.

Democratic Assembly Speaker Anthony J. Travia is opposed to the bill, but has said he will put it up for debate. Republican Senate Majority Leader Earl W. Brydges is against the bill, but has made no promises that the measure will even get out of committee. Lieut. Gov. Malcolm L. Wilson's opposition to the bill is even more adamant than that of the legislative leaders, and the state's Catholic bishops are also expected to persist in their opposition to revision.

Thus the prospects for major overhaul of the law this year are slight, and for moderate change, only somewhat better.

Abortion and Sterilization Win Support of Planned Parenthood

BY MORRIS KAPLAN | NOV. 14, 1968

FOR THE FIRST TIME in its 52 years as a national voluntary birth-control agency, Planned Parenthood-World Population yesterday approved unanimously a policy recognizing abortion and sterilization as proper medical procedures. It called for liberalizing the criminal laws that prohibit them.

An individual is now liable in almost all states to prosecution under the criminal code if he participates in an abortion except to save the mother's life. Less restrictive measures have been passed recently in Colorado, California, Maryland, North Carolina and the District of Columbia.

The 650 representatives of 158 affiliated Planned Parenthood groups in 37 states and the District of Columbia endorsed the new policy at a conference in the Roosevelt Hotel. But the ratification will not be binding on the affiliates until each decides.

The organization elected Dr. Jerome H. Holland, sociologist and president of Hampton Institute, as its chairman. He is the first Negro in the post. The 52-year-old native of Auburn, N. Y. is a graduate of Cornell University, where he was an All-America end on the football team.

Dr. Holland pledged his support for the group's program, saying that those who call birth control a form of genocide "are not aware of the real meaning of family planning and its uses."

The Pittsburgh branch of the National Association for the Advancement of Colored People last year criticized family planners as bent on trying to keep the Negro birth rate as low as possible.

The birth-control agency reaffirmed that abortion is a medical procedure and a decision that must rest with the woman and her physician. This decision, the committee said, should be made with full knowledge of the woman's personal situation and with consideration of her social, economic and cultural environment.

Dr. Alan F. Guttmacher, an obstetrician and gynecologist who has been president of the Planned Parenthood group since 1963, expressed pleasure that the group had taken a positive stand on "the necessity to liberalize" abortion and sterilization statutes.

NOT ROUTINE CONTROL

He cautioned, however, that neither procedure should take the place of effective contraception. His group believes, he said, that abortion and sterilization "are medically and socially desirable only in unusual circumstances, never for routine birth control."

Dr. Guttmacher was a pro-reform member of Governor Rockefeller's committee to recommend changes in the state's 85-year-old abortion law in time for action by the last Legislature. The lawmakers voted down the reform bill introduced by Assemblyman Albert H. Blumenthal, a Manhattan Reform Democrat.

Delegates voted yesterday to accept recommendations of their 100-member board of directors, which had confirmed overwhelmingly the policy of the organization's national medical advisory committee. The latter held that it was the right and responsibility of every woman to decide whether and when to have a child.

It reaffirmed that abortion is a medical procedure and a decision that must rest with the woman and her physician. The committee added that this decision should be made with full knowledge of the woman's personal situation, with consideration of her social, economic and cultural environment.

The committee recommended the abolition of existing laws and criminal laws regarding abortion and the recognition that advice, counseling and referral constituted an integral part of medical care.

It called voluntary sterilization of either man or woman a medically accepted means of permanent conception control. It urged that legal restrictions be removed and that the individual be given the right to decide the course to follow with his or her physician. It recommended also that Planned Parenthood centers offer appropriate information and referral.

The board of directors stressed its support of voluntarism in the matter and condemned "any kind of overt or subvert coercion."

A spokesman said that the board had recognized that safe, legal abortion must be available in some situations as "a back-up medical technique." The spokesman pointed out that although the contraceptive pill was virtually 100 per cent effective "many women forget and any interruption in the schedule could lead to pregnancy."

Roe v. Wade and the Evolution of Abortion Law

The Supreme Court's landmark decision in the case of Roe v. Wade marked a definitive turning point in U.S. history for a woman's right to privacy and, by extension, her right to seek an abortion. It set a legal precedent that would dominate the public discourse on abortion for decades to come. Legislation in individual U.S. states was also under more scrutiny than ever before. Elected officials struggled with the particulars of providing or banning abortion services and even began to weigh in on questions such as: When does life begin?

National Guidelines Set by 7-to-2 Vote

BY WARREN WEAVER JR. | **JAN. 23, 1973**

WASHINGTON, JAN. 22 — The Supreme Court overruled today all state laws that prohibit or restrict a woman's right to obtain an abortion during her first three months of pregnancy. The vote was 7 to 2.

In a historic resolution of a fiercely controversial issue, the Court drafted a new set of national guidelines that will result in broadly liberalized anti-abortion laws in 46 states but will not abolish restrictions altogether.

Establishing an unusually detailed timetable for the relative legal rights of pregnant women and the states that would control their acts, the majority specified the following:

- For the first three months of pregnancy the decision to have an abortion lies with the woman and her doctor, and the state's interest in her welfare is not "compelling" enough to warrant any interference.

- For the next six months of pregnancy a state may "regulate the abortion procedure in ways that are reasonably related to maternal health," such as licensing and regulating the persons and facilities involved.

- For the last 10 weeks of pregnancy, the period during which the fetus is judged to be capable of surviving if born, any state may prohibit abortions, if it wishes, except where they may be necessary to preserve the life or health of the mother.

Today's action will not affect existing laws in New York, Alaska, Hawaii and Washington, where abortions are now legally available in the early months of pregnancy. But it will require rewriting of statutes in every other state.

The basic Texas case decided by the Court today will invalidate strict anti-abortion laws in 31 states; a second decision involving Georgia will require considerable rewriting of more liberal statutes in 15 others.

Justice Harry A. Blackmun wrote the majority opinion in which Chief Justice Warren E. Burger and Justices William O. Douglas, William J. Brennan Jr., Potter Stewart, Thurgood Marshall and Lewis F. Powell Jr. joined.

Dissenting were Justices Byron R. White and William H. Rehnquist.

Justice White, calling the decision "an exercise of raw judicial power," wrote that "the Court apparently values the convenience of the pregnant mother more than the continued existence and development of the life or potential life which she carries."

The Court's decision was at odds with the expressed views of President Nixon. Last May, in a letter to Cardinal Cooke, he opposed "liberalized abortion policies" and spoke out for "the right to life of literally hundreds of thousands of unborn children."

But three of the four Justices Mr. Nixon has appointed to the Supreme Court voted with the majority, with only Mr. Rehnquist dissenting.

The majority rejected the idea that a fetus becomes a "person" upon conception and is thus entitled to the due process and equal protection guarantees of the Constitution. This view was pressed by opponents of liberalized abortion, including the Roman Catholic Church.

Justice Blackmun concluded that "the word 'person,' as used in the 14th Amendment, does not include the unborn," although states may acquire, "at some point in time" of pregnancy, an interest in the "potential human life" that the fetus represents, to permit regulation.

It is that interest, the Court said, that permits states to prohibit abortion during the last 10 weeks of pregnancy, after the fetus has developed the capacity to survive.

In both cases decided today, the plaintiffs had based their protest on an assertion that state laws limiting the availability of abortion had circumscribed rights and freedoms guaranteed them by the Constitution: due process of law, equal protection of the laws, freedom of action and a particular privacy involving a personal and family matter.

In its decision on the challenge to the Georgia abortion law, the high court majority struck down several requirements that a woman seeking to terminate her pregnancy in that state would have to meet.

DECISION FOR DOCTORS

Among them were a flat prohibition on abortions for out-of-state residents and requirements that hospitals be accredited by a private agency, that applicants be screened by a hospital committee and that two independent doctors certify the potential danger to the applicant's health.

The Georgia law permitted abortions when a doctor found in "his best clinical judgment" that continued pregnancy would threaten the woman's life or health, that the fetus would be likely to be born defective or that the pregnancy was the result of rape.

The same Supreme Court majority, with Justice Blackmun writing the opinion again, emphasized that this medical judgment should cover all relevant factors — "physical, emotional, psychological familial and the woman's age."

In some of the 15 states with laws similar to Georgia's, doctors have tended to take a relatively narrow view of what constituted a woman's health in deciding whether an abortion was legally justified.

The Texas law that the Court invalidated entirely was typical of the criminal statutes passed in the last half of the 19th century prohibiting all abortions except those to save a mother's life. The Georgia law, approved in 1972 and altered by the Court today, was patterned after the model penal code of the American Law Institute.

In the Texas case, Justice Blackmun wrote that the constitutional right of privacy, developed by the Court in a long series of decisions, was "broad enough to encompass a woman's decision whether or not to terminate her pregnancy."

He rejected, however, the argument of women's rights groups that this right was absolute "and she is entitled to terminate her pregnancy at whatever time, in whatever way and for whatever reason she alone chooses."

"With this we do not agree," the Justice declared.

"A state may properly assert important interests in safeguarding health, in maintaining medical standards and in protecting potential life," Mr. Blackmun observed. "At some point in pregnancy, these respective interests become sufficiently compelling to sustain regulation of the factors that govern the abortion decision."

The majority concluded that this "compelling" state interest arose at the end of the first three months of pregnancy because of the "now established medical fact" that until then, fewer women die from abortions than from normal childbirth.

During this three-month period, the Court said, a doctor can recommend an abortion to his patient "without regulation by the state" and the resulting operations can be conducted "free of interference by the state."

The "compelling state interest" in the fetus does not arise, however, until the time of "viability," Justice Blackmun wrote, when it has "the capability of meaningful life outside the mother's womb." This occurs about 10 weeks before delivery.

In reading an abbreviated version of his two opinions to the Court this morning, Justice Blackmun noted that most state legislatures were in session now and would thus be able to rewrite their states' abortion laws to conform to the Court's decision.

Both of today's cases wound up with anonymous parties winning victories over state officials. In the Texas case, "Jane Roe," an unmarried pregnant woman who was allowed to bring the case without further identity, was the only plaintiff after the Supreme Court disqualified a doctor and a childless couple who said that the wife's health would be endangered by pregnancy.

In the Georgia case, the surviving plaintiff was "Mary Doe," who, when she brought the action, was a 22-year-old married woman 11 weeks pregnant with her fourth child.

Excerpts From Abortion Case

SPECIAL TO THE NEW YORK TIMES | JAN. 23, 1973

WASHINGTON, JAN. 22 — Following are excerpts from the majority opinion, written by Justice Harry A. Blackmun, in Jane Roe v. Henry Wade, the Texas abortion case, and from the dissent written by Justice Byron R. White:

MAJORITY OPINION

The Texas statutes under attack here are typical of those that have been in effect in many states for approximately a century. These make it a crime to "procure an abortion," as therein defined, or to attempt one, except with respect to "an abortion procured or attempted by medical advice for the purpose of saving the life of the mother." Similar statutes are in existence in a majority of the states.

It perhaps is not generally appreciated that the restrictive criminal abortion laws in effect in a majority of states are of relatively recent vintage. Instead, they derive from statutory changes effected, for the most part, in the latter half of the 19th century.

When most criminal abortion laws were first enacted, the procedure was a hazardous one for the woman.

PRIVACY RIGHTS UNCLEAR

The Constitution does not explicitly mention any right of privacy. In a line of decisions, however, the Court has recognized that a right of personal privacy, or a guarantee of certain areas or zones of privacy, does exist under the Constitution.

This right of privacy, whether it be founded in the 14th Amendment's concept of personal liberty and restrictions upon state action, as we feel it is, or, as the District Court determined, in the Ninth Amendment's reservation of rights to the people, is broad enough to encompass a woman's decision whether or not to terminate her pregnancy.

The detriment that the state would impose upon the pregnant woman by denying this choice altogether is apparent. Specific and direct harm medically diagnosable even in early pregnancy may be involved. Maternity, or additional offspring, may force upon the woman a distressful life and future. Psychological harm may be imminent. Mental and physical wealth may be taxed by child care.

There is also the distress, for all concerned, associated with the unwanted child, and there is the problem of bringing a child into a family already unable, psychologically and otherwise, to care for it.

On the basis of elements such as these, appellants and some amici argue that the woman's right is absolute and that she is entitled to terminate her pregnancy at whatever time, in whatever way, and for whatever reason she alone chooses. With this we do not agree.

The Court's decision recognizing a right of privacy also acknowledges that some state regulation in areas protected by that right is appropriate. A state may properly assert important interests in safeguarding health, in maintaining medical standards and in protecting potential life.

At the same point in pregnancy, these respective interests become sufficiently compelling to sustain regulation of the factors that govern the abortion decision.

The appellee and certain amici argue that the fetus is a "person" within the language and meaning of the 14th Amendment. In support of this they outline at length and in detail the well-known facts of fetal development. If this suggestion of parenthood is established, the appellant's case, of course, collapses, for the fetus' right to life is then guaranteed specifically by the amendment.

The Constitution does not define "person" in so many words. The use of the word is such that it has application only postnatally.

All this, together with our observation that throughout the major portion of the 19th century prevailing legal abortion practices were far freer than they are today, persuades us that the word "person," as used in the 14th Amendment, does not include the unborn.

Justice Harry A. Blackmun.

Texas urges that, apart from the 14th Amendment, life begins at conception and is present throughout pregnancy, and that, therefore, the state has a compelling interest in protecting that life from and after conception.

We need not resolve the difficult question of when life begins. When those trained in the respective disciplines of medicine, philosophy and theology are unable to arrive at any consensus, the judiciary, at this point in the development of man's knowledge, is not in a position to speculate as to the answer.

The unborn have never been recognized in the law as persons in the whole sense.

With respect to the state's important and legitimate interest in the health of the mother, the "compelling" point, in the light of present medical knowledge, is at approximately the end of the first trimester. This is so because of the now established medical fact that until the end of the first trimester mortality in abortion is less than mortality in normal childbirth.

It follows that, from and after this point, a state may regulate the abortion procedure to the extent that the regulation reasonably relates to the preservation and protection of maternal health.

With respect to the state's important and legitimate interest in potential life, the "compelling" point is at viability. This is so because the fetus then presumably has the capability of meaningful life outside the mother's womb. If the state is interested in protecting fetal life after viability, it may go so far as to proscribe abortion during that period except when it is necessary to preserve the life or health of the mother.

DISSENTING OPINION

At the heart of the controversy in these cases are those recurring pregnancies that pose no danger whatsoever to the life or health of the mother but are nevertheless unwanted for any one or more of a variety of reasons — convenience, family planning, economics, dislike of children, the embarrassment of illegitimacy, etc.

The common claim before us is that for any one of such reasons, or for no reason at all, and without asserting or claiming any threat to life or health, any woman is entitled to an abortion at her request if she is able to find a medical adviser willing to undertake the procedure.

The Court for the most part sustains this position during the period prior to the time the fetus becomes viable, the Constitution of the United States values the convenience, whim or caprice of the putative mother more than life or potential life of the fetus.

The upshot is that the people and the legislatures of the 50 states are constitutionally disentitled to weigh the relative importance of the continued existence and development of the fetus on the one hand against a spectrum of possible impacts on the mother on the other hand.

As an exercise of raw judicial Power, the Court perhaps has authority to do what it does today; but in my view its judgment is an improvident and extravagant exercise of the power of judicial review which the constitution extends to this court.

I find no constitutional warrant for imposing such an order of priorities on the people and legislatures of the states. In a sensitive area such as this, involving as it does issues over which reasonable men may easily and heatedly differ, I cannot accept the Court's exercise of its clear power of choice by interposing a constitutional barrier to state efforts to protect human life and by investing mothers and doctors with the constitutionally protected right to exterminate it. This issue, for the most part, should be left with the people and to the political processes the people have devised to their affairs.

The Supreme Court as Moral Arbiter

OPINION | BY DANIEL A. DEGNAN | MARCH 10, 1973

SYRACUSE, N. Y. — As a citizen of the United States, a Catholic priest and a teacher of law, I was not only shocked by the U.S. Supreme Court's recent decision on abortion, but I felt oddly reduced by it. I shall try to explain why.

Last year I conducted a seminar on problems in law and morals, touching, a bit loosely at times, on questions ranging from civil disobedience and privacy to genetic control and abortion. We spent almost a month on abortion and the law, however. Among the members of the seminar, positions on abortion covered the spectrum.

For one thing, we had to consider the sources and quality of the different arguments concerning the morality of abortion and its implications for law. For another, we explored positions, such as Thomas Aquinas', that law should not attempt to restrain all immoral acts, but only the graver ones, since if law attempted to restrain all such acts it would be ineffective and the common good of the political community itself would he injured. Although abortion is considered by many to be a gravely immoral act, one had to add that in a pluralistic society faced by division and uncertainty over the morality of abortion, the law might have to reflect some compromise.

That was last year, however. In the case of Roe v. Wade, decided on Jan. 22, the Supreme Court of the United States has declared (1) that a constitutional right of personal privacy entitles a woman to terminate her pregnancy by an abortion, (2) this right is a right to noninterference by the law during the first six months of pregnancy (except for some health regulations) because the state has no compelling interest in the life of the fetus during that time, and (3) after viability of the fetus (in the 24th to 28th week), the personal right to an abortion can be limited by the state's power to require that the abortion be necessary for the life health of the woman.

In the Court's peculiar language, when the fetus has the capability of "meaningful life" outside the mother's womb, the state's interest in potential life is "compelling" enough to allow the state to "go so far as to proscribe abortion during that period except when it is necessary to preserve the life or health of the mother." The health of the mother is so broadly defined in the companion case of Doe v. Bolton that it amounts to a judgment of a physician that an abortion is indicated. The judgment appears to be entrusted to any physician, including one who serves in an abortion clinic.

The Supreme Court has decided the moral and legal issues I had thought so serious and so difficult for society. The decision comes in the guise of legal question, a constitutional right of privacy, but if the only question had been the privacy of the woman, we could all have gone home long ago.

Those who believe that the state should prohibit or restrict abortions have insisted that a fetus is human life or at least potential human life and that, as with all human life, the law should respect and protect it.

Just as the old "freedom of contract" turned the Constitution into a barrier against social legislation, the new right of personal privacy bars laws protecting the fetus. The Court's opinion in Roe v. Wade made much of saying that the arguments against abortion were based upon "one theory of life," but the Court has now erected into constitutional law its own theory of fetal life. The Court's theory, simply stated, is that fetal life, even to the moment of birth, has only the barest claim to protection (if any) when measured against a woman's right to terminate her pregnancy.

Since the seminar last year, my own position on abortion has included a deep concern for the life of the fetus, especially as the fetus advanced toward birth, and a conviction that our society must have moderate laws aimed at recognizing and protecting fetal life while not prohibiting all abortions.

I expected to work for amendment of the New York law, which allowed abortions on demand up to twenty-four weeks. Even an eighteen-week limit, I thought, would help to prevent live babies from being left to die after an abortion. I hoped and expected that the people of New York and the nation would react against the excesses of the pro-abortion movement and of course I thought that I would have, as a citizen, the opportunity to try to convince my fellow Americans of this position.

But the Supreme Court has spoken and these concerns for the protection of potential human life by the law cannot be advanced anymore. I cannot hope that the law will vindicate them. Acting as moral arbiter for me and my fellow citizens, the Court has decided with precision the relative value of fetal life in an abortion and has foreclosed for us one of the profound issues of our time. That is why the decision is not only shocking; it reduces us. We are not children and the Supreme Court is not our moral arbiter.

THE REV. DANIEL A. DEGNAN, a member of the Jesuit order, is also a lawyer. He teaches law at Syracuse University.

As Congressmen Take Up the Abortion Issue, Two Sides Debate: When Does Life Begin?

BY THE NEW YORK TIMES | APRIL 19, 1981

EIGHT YEARS AGO, in the landmark Roe v. Wade ruling, the Supreme Court legalized abortion during the first stages of pregnancy. Since then, opponents have been seeking a way to undo that decision, which was based on the woman's right to privacy. Since a constitutional amendment to outlaw abortion seems unattainable, abortion opponents have introduced a bill in Congress, S. 158, which declares that human life 'shall be deemed to exist from conception,' thus allowing states, if they choose, to prosecute abortion as murder. The bill is based on a clause of the 14th Amendment that gives Congress the power to enforce the Amendment's due process and equal protection guarantees. Hearings on it begin this week.

The Week in Review asked Senator Orrin G. Hatch, a Utah Republican and abortion foe who heads the Senate Judiciary Subcommittee on the Constitution, and Rhonda Copelon, a lawyer with the Center for Constitutional Rights in New York and a proponent of legal abortions, to discuss the merits of the bill and its implications. Excerpts from their interviews with Robert Reinhold, a Washington reporter for The New York Times, follow.

ORRIN G. HATCH

Question. *Do you think that a Congressional statute is the proper approach to this issue?*

Senator Hatch. Well, I continue to prefer a constitutional amendment to deal with the Roe v. Wade decision. I am not yet entirely comfortable with S.158, the statutory approach, but I do believe that a credible case can be made for it. I'm strongly committed to the 'right to life' effort, and the need in Congress to overturn Roe; but I am equally committed to a sound constitutional approach.

Section 5 of the 14th Amendment, however, gives Congress the power to enforce by appropriate legislation the provisions of the 14th Amendment. S.158 would make the Congressional finding that human life shall be deemed to exist from the point of conception, without regard to race, age, health, defect or condition of dependency. It would make the further finding that "a person," for purposes of the due process guarantees of the 14th Amendment, would include all human life.

Q. *Would it not be possible to nullify many Supreme Court decisions just by changing definitions of a word?*

A. If it is extended in a very broad sense, it would permit legislative circumvention in some Supreme Court decisions. But keep in mind that those on the other side of this issue didn't mind going around the 14th Amendment to have their issues resolved by Congress. I frankly think it's ironic that the liberals applauded decisions like Katzenbach v. Morgan (which struck down literacy tests in voting) and Fullilove v. Klutznick (upholding affirmative action in racial hiring) when they were handed down, because they granted extensive powers to Congress.

Now those decisions are the law of the land and S.158 is the conservative response. Or, should I say, the family-oriented response to the liberals who want it both ways. They want to be able to circumvent the 14th Amendment anytime they wish, but when the family-oriented people, who feel that abortion is an insidiously bad thing, want to come out with S.158, there is a hue and a cry that, 'Oh, my goodness, you can't do this.' Now I think that what's sauce for the goose is sauce for the gander.

CLARIFICATIONS AND COMPROMISES

Q. *Would the law require states to punish a rape victim seeking an abortion as a murderer? Or the druggist who sold her a morning-after pill as an accomplice?*

A. I think that is something that would have to be resolved afterwards.

Q. *Afterwards?*

A. After the passage of the bill, assuming it passes.

Q. *Some people would argue that you shouldn't leave those kinds of loose ends.*

A. Well, unfortunately, the law always does leave loose ends because there's no way of absolutely determining how a particular law is going to be interpreted by any of the courts, including the Supreme Court. We've always found some astounding decisions by the Supreme Court.

Q. *With the advances in biological sciences, such as test tube conceptions, we've blurred the point at which life starts. Doesn't this law create a morass of questions about defining that point?*

A. No, S.158 would resolve that ambiguity. It says that life begins at conception.

Q. *Would life include something created in a lab?*

A. That would have to be determined under this statute as it is written; I presume that it probably would.

Q. *You'd determine that by interpretation?*

A. Yes. Our committee intends to explore all of these questions. We're willing to listen to experts in many areas; however, I don't know that even experts will resolve the question of 'when does life begin?'

Q. *Do you personally believe the law should apply even to victims of rape and incest?*

A. I think we would have a much better chance of getting it through the Congress if those two exceptions were put in. I personally prefer the constitutional amendment. That makes no exception except to save the life of the mother. But on the other hand, let's face it, the amendment to the Medicaid funding, which was already on the books, did provide for abortions to save the life of the mother and for rape or incest. Those of us who believe in the sanctity of human life were not totally happy with that, but we thought it was better than leaving it up to bureaucrats which human life can be taken and using federal dollars to have indiscriminate abortions all over America. I believe we should do whatever we can to protect the sanctity of human life. If that's as far as we can go, then I'd rather do that than not have any protection.

Q. *Doesn't this bill use the law to impose religious and moral views of one group on others?*

A. One does not have to hold any particular religious view to examine and make conclusions with respect to biological evidence on the beginning of life. And, as the Supreme Court noted in Harris v. McCrae, legislation relating to abortion is not necessarily in violation of the First Amendment simply because it's consistent with the doctrines of some, or all, religions.

Q. *Some would argue that the sponsors of this bill are doing it mainly for the political purpose of satisfying the anti-abortion forces.*

A. I know the sponsors of the bill and they're very sincere and dedicated. I think there is no such consideration.

Q. *The reason that this bill was introduced was that the sponsors did not get an amendment through. What are the chances, in your view, of its passage?*

A. I think it has an excellent chance. I believe that this is one of the great constitutional debates of this century. The courts have said that it's basically not a religious question. To those who are antagonistic toward indiscriminate abortion, it is in some respects a religious question and certainly a family-oriented question. I think that this particular debate could resolve those issues by just making the simple determination of when life begins. And if Congress has that power, then S.158 may be the way for those who are against abortion, including myself, to resolve this very volatile and difficult issue.

RHONDA COPELON

Question. *Is a statute the proper way to deal with this issue?*

Miss Copelon. No. The only way you can reverse Roe v. Wade is through a Constitutional amendment. But even a constitutional amendment would be a tragedy, not only for women but for the country.

Q. *Nevertheless, if the Congressional law were passed, what would be its practical consequences?*

A. It would mean, first of all, that states could criminalize abortion if they wanted to. And since the statute attempts to make an equation between a fetus and a person under the Constitution, it would be at least permissible and possibly required to treat abortion as equal to homicide, which includes murder and manslaughter.

A statute or an amendment would not, as its proponents say, simply return us to the situation before Roe. Before that, abortion was a minor form felony, a separate crime. The old laws had to do with the medical dangers of abortion. The declaration of the fetus as a legal person has no reference point in any constitution law, common, or statutory law.

Q. *What effects would you anticipate from the recriminalization of abortion?*

A. It would have a very significant impact on women's health, not only because women would be forced to turn to dangerous illegal abortions, but because doctors would be reluctant to provide care for medical complications of abortion or of miscarriage, because of fear of investigation. Certain kinds of birth control would be threatened and potentially outlawed.

Moreover, criminalization would bring into play severe penalties not only for women but for those was assist them in getting abortions. It would generate a surveillance and enforcement process which, to succeed, would have to intrude on the most intimate aspects of a person's life. For example, every miscarriage would have to be investigated. Was it induced abortion or a spontaneous one? Did it happen because the woman failed to provide maximum protection to the embryo?

Q. *Do you believe the people pursing this bill would take it to such extremes?*

A. Yes. One has to recognize that underlying the drive is a religious-moral position. When you enact a law at the behest of a religiously motivated movement, you have the potential for the most extreme application. A good example is Prohibition, which started with an attack on public drunkenness and ended up making constitutionally illegal the most minimum form of alcoholized beer. It ended up trying to impose a morality through a criminal statute which had been given the force of the Constitution. That is a real danger. Most of the people who want to treat abortion as a severe crime really want to see all abortions ferreted out.

UNDERLYING PREMISES

Q. *What is their motive, in your view?*

A. I think the underlying motive is an attack on women, on their right to self-determination which is at the core of being human and on their right to be sexual apart from procreation. If there is no abortion, every act of sex is an act of fear. I also see it as a mechanism for excluding women from certain workplaces.

Q. *Why is that?*

A. We have just come out of a period in the last 10 years of thinking about women as fragile vessels during pregnancy. A law declaring a fetus a person would imply that while you are pregnant, your activities are subservient to the primary goal of insuring that pregnancy survives. Working in a job that requires physical exertion could easily be seen as creating some risk to the fetus.

Q. *Do you recognize no rights of the fetus?*

A. Roe v. Wade says that under the 14th Amendment the fetus is not a legal person entitled to claim civil rights for itself. It also says that the question of when human life begins is a moral issue about which there are deep philosophical and theological differences. Underpinning the Court's refusal in Roe to allow states to adopt a theory of life is the pluralistic premise that in our society, people have the right to hold different beliefs and to live in accordance with those beliefs. The law enforces a moral norm only when there is a consensus.

Q. *Wouldn't different states be able to interpret the law differently?*

A. The proponents of the bill want to call it a states' rights approach. But if they were able to sustain a declaration of fetal personhood in a statute, they could try to enforce it in the states through individual lawsuits brought by people who style themselves as guardians of fetuses. Also, any public money for provision of abortion would surely be challenged. For example, in New York State, which voluntarily funds abortions for the poor, such funds could be stopped.

Q. *If the enforcement provision of the 14th Amendment can be used to enforce voting rights and affirmative action, why can't it be used by abortion foes?*

A. The basic power of Congress under Section 5 (of the 14th Amendment) is to provide remedies for discrimination. This bill is not an exercise of that power. It is an exercise of a power that Congress does not have, to reinterpret the Constitution. Roe v. Wade correctly said that under the 14th Amendment, the word "person" does not apply to prenatal life. They are now trying to redefine the word in the 14th Amendment. If Congress can enact this law, it could enact a law again which holds that "equal" means "separate but equal." It could use its power to reverse every Supreme Court decision that the current majority in Congress does not like.

Q. *If passed, will such a law be struck down by the Supreme Court?*

A. I think it is such an unconstitutional statute, and such a direct assault on the fundamental role of the Court that they would lose their role in our system if they sustained it. On the other hand, one has to take into account that the political pressures are very extreme. Underlying this statute is an attempt to create a political confrontation between Congress and the courts, to create a constitutional crisis.

Contempt for Abortion, and Tolerance

EDITORIAL | **BY THE NEW YORK TIMES** | **JAN. 27, 1986**

LAST WEEK MARKED the 13th anniversary of Roe v. Wade, the Supreme Court decision that legalized abortion, and Washington was once more the scene of the "March for Life" rally. The crowd was only half what it was last year, but the enthusiasm was the same — and so was the host. "We will continue to work together with Congress," President Ronald Reagan told the crowd, "to overturn the tragedy of Roe v. Wade."

The Supreme Court decision does not endorse abortion; it leaves up to a woman and her doctor the choice to continue a pregnancy, at least during the first trimester. It allows some limitation on abortion in the second trimester and even greater limitation in the third. Nonetheless, many Americans oppose the decision, some so strenuously that they line the entrances to abortion clinics harassing and hissing the patients. Often, by letter and telephone, they threaten bombs and arson. Sometimes they follow through.

The abortion argument didn't begin with Roe v. Wade, however. It has divided humankind for centuries, and probably always will. One side of the debate finds abortion a morally indefensible destruction of life; the other finds forcing a woman to incubate a fetus against her will an equally immoral invasion of her right to control her body. Roe v. Wade made clear that however passionate the debate, neither side has the superior moral claim.

Instead, Justice Blackmun held that a woman's rights must be weighed against the fetus's growing potential for life. From this he reasoned that the state's interest in protecting life increases as the fetus grows closer to term. That profoundly humane effort to accommodate deep moral conflicts was in the finest American tradition of tolerance.

Mr. Reagan's long opposition to abortion made predictable his welcome to the demonstrators, followed by his advice, quoted by a member of the National Right to Life Committee, that an end to violence would earn their movement "a lot of brownie points." Surely millions of Americans hoped for something more from a President, especially one whose fondest promise was to get the Government off people's backs. This was, after all, the anniversary of a Supreme Court decision that gave practical voice not to abortion or to its foes but to tolerance and liberty.

Legal Abortion Under Fierce Attack 15 Years After Roe v. Wade Ruling

BY TAMAR LEWIN | MAY 10, 1988

FIFTEEN YEARS AFTER the United States Supreme Court ruled that women have a constitutional right to abortion, groups on both sides of the issue say that right is increasingly vulnerable to attack.

The changing makeup of the Supreme Court since the 7-to-2 ruling in the case, Roe v. Wade, is the most obvious sign of that vulnerability. Newcomers to the Court since the 1973 ruling are generally thought to oppose abortion, and those who support abortion rights are among the oldest Justices.

While several states have imposed restrictions of one kind or another since Roe v. Wade was decided, it appears now that anti-abortion groups are actively trying to set the stage for a Supreme Court reconsideration of the fundamental issue.

"Up until now, the anti-choice groups have been chipping away at the right to abortion with a chisel," said Kate Michelman, executive director of the National Abortion Rights Action League. "But now, they've picked up a sledgehammer, and they're trying to crush the whole thing. They obviously feel that it is within their reach to over-turn Roe v. Wade, and make abortion illegal again. And the frightening thing is that I'm not sure they're wrong."

THE LINES ARE DRAWN

Although it is impossible to predict how each Justice would rule in any particular case, four of the current Justices — William J. Brennan Jr., Thurgood Marshall, Harry A. Blackmun and John Paul Stevens — are generally considered supportive of the right to have an abortion.

Four others, Chief Justice William H. Rehnquist and Justices Antonin Scalia, Sandra Day O'Connor and Byron R. White, are widely considered to be against abortion. Indeed, Justices Rehnquist and

White were the dissenters in the 1973 decision. The views on the issue of the newest justice, Anthony M. Kennedy, are unclear.

Since three of the Justices believed to support abortion rights will be in their 80's by the time the next President is elected, that count could well shift.

The Court's 5-to-4 vote late last month to reconsider an important 1976 civil rights ruling may have been another harbinger.

"If the majority of the Court wants to reopen and rethink the interpretation of the civil rights laws, you have to wonder how long it's going to be before they want to take another look at Roe v. Wade," Ms. Michelman said.

Anti-abortion groups are fighting to overturn Roe v. Wade in the courts, on the streets and in state legislatures. In the last week of April, the Arizona Legislature voted twice on a bill that would have banned all abortions except those needed to save the life of a woman. While the bill, the broadest challenge since Roe v. Wade, failed to pass each time by a single vote, those concerned with abortion said it was significant that legislation directly challenging the decision was taken seriously.

OTHER RECENT DEVELOPMENTS

Also distressing to abortion-rights activists and, in equal measure, heartening to the anti-abortion groups, are several other developments, including these:

• A recent spate of lower-court cases asserting that fathers-to-be should have some rights to prevent women from having abortions.

• The difficult fight earlier this year over the Reagan Administration's attempt to end Federal financing for clinics that offer abortion counseling.

• The continuing legal skirmishes over state laws requiring notification of the parents of a minor seeking an abortion, or other obstacles to an immediate abortion.

So far, the abortion-rights groups have fended off every major challenge. But the bitterness of the fight has not ebbed at all. Anti-abortion demonstrations and efforts to block women from entering clinics that perform abortions — including a series of protests in and around New York City last week that resulted in hundreds of arrests — are, if anything, escalating.

"There's no question that we feel a new energizing on the part of the right-to-lifers," said Janet Benshoof of the American Civil Liberties Union's Reproductive Freedom Project. "I think it's because we're seeing the Court change before our eyes, and because we've had an anti-abortion Administration in office for almost eight years."

REAGAN HAS PLAYED ROLE

President Reagan has helped the anti-abortion movement in several ways, from appointments that have made the Federal judiciary considerably more conservative to the regulations, recently declared unconstitutional by courts, ending Federal financing for clinics that provide abortion counseling or referrals.

"Having the chief executive of the leading nation in the world work with us to keep the Federal Government out of the abortion business has been very important," said David O'Steen, executive director of the National Right-to-Life Committee.

With advances in medical technology, the debate has expanded to encompass other ethical questions, including the medical use of fetal tissue. Anti-abortion groups, by threatening a boycott, even prevented American pharmaceutical companies from importing a new drug, RU 486, that medical researchers say is for many women a safe alternative to surgical abortions. In a new book put out by the National Right-to-Life Committee, "A Passion for Justice," Dr. J. C. Willke, the Cincinnati physician who founded the organization, writes that "almost all signs now point toward" the limitation or abolition of the right to abortion.

Dr. Willke's opponents concede that his group has been very successful in shifting the abortion debate away from the question of women's rights, and refocusing it, instead, on the fetus, with frequent references to the "tiny heartbeat" that can be found six or seven weeks after conception, or the sight on an ultrasound screen of an eight-week fetus that appears to be sucking its thumb in the womb.

"Even though polls show that most Americans support the right to abortion, the anti-abortion side has in some way won the public debate, captured the terms and framed the issues," said Ms. Michelman. "There is very little discussion these days about how every dimension of a woman's life is influenced by the right to reproductive freedom. We have to remind people that abortion is the guarantor of a woman's full right to choose and her right to participate fully in the social and political life of society."

Anti-abortion groups say the 1973 decision was so poorly reasoned that the high court is bound to repudiate it.

"Roe is based on medical ignorance and legal ignorance," said Mr. O'Steen. "Now that we can see the unborn child swimming in the womb on an ultrasound screen, no one can stand up with a straight face and argue that life doesn't begin at the moment of fertilization."

Even many feminist legal scholars say privately that the legal reasoning in the decision was flawed and, therefore, may prove easier than they would like to overturn.

In Roe v. Wade, Justice Blackmun found that the right to abortion was part of the right to privacy — a mushy legal area, not mentioned anywhere in the Constitution — and that until a fetus becomes viable, toward the end of the second trimester of pregnancy, the state may not intrude on a woman's decision to have an abortion.

Abortion-rights lawyers say the right to abortion would be far safer if the court had, instead, analyzed it as part of a better-established Constitutional right, such as equality or liberty or the avoidance of involuntary servitude.

"What we need now is a second-generation body of law, expanding on Roe v. Wade," Ms. Michelman said.

What Is Right and Wrong With Roe v. Wade?

BY LAURA MANSNERUS | APRIL 23, 1989

The view from friends of the court.

IN THE ABORTION CASE it will hear on Wednesday, the Supreme Court could simply consider whether the restrictions in Missouri's law violate the guidelines of Roe v. Wade, the 1973 decision that legalized abortion. But it could also consider, as both the state and the Bush Administration have asked it to do, whether Roe v. Wade should survive at all.

That possibility has made Webster v. Reproductive Health Services the most closely watched abortion case since 1973. And given the erosion of the majority that issued Roe v. Wade, people on both sides of the issue are more eager than ever to make their arguments. In the Missouri case, which is not so different from many others it has heard, the Court has received 78 friend-of-the-court briefs, 20 more than were ever before submitted for a single case.

The legal reasoning of Roe has come under attack before, but the decision has stood largely undisturbed, and the Court has reaffirmed it in several recent opinions. To abortion-rights proponents, anything less was — until the Webster case — practically unthinkable.

The Roe decision was based on the "concept of personal liberty" in the 14th Amendment, which forbids a state to "deprive any person of life, liberty or property without due process of law." This right of privacy, Justice Harry A. Blackmun wrote, "is broad enough to encompass a woman's decision whether or not to terminate her pregnancy."

Thus the right to abortion, like the right to marry or to raise one's own children, was recognized as a "fundamental right" under the Constitution. These can be curtailed only when the state has a "compelling interest" in doing so. Generally speaking, if no fundamental right is at stake, any kind of state regulation will be upheld so long as it has a rational basis.

Demonstrators at a pro-choice march in April 1989.

The Court outlined a three-stage approach: Some regulation of abortion is allowed after the first trimester, and more after the second trimester — at which point, the Court said, the fetus is viable and the state's interest in protecting it becomes compelling.

The Missouri law requires a physician to conduct tests for viability if the woman requesting the abortion appears to be 20 or more weeks pregnant. It also bars abortions at public clinics or hospitals, even when the woman pays the entire bill, and prohibits the use of public funds for abortion counseling.

The Court could rule on these provisions, as it has with more than a dozen other state abortion laws, by applying the guidelines it set out in 1973. To do so would effectively be reaffirming Roe. But the Court could at the same time narrow its own rule, giving the states more leeway in their abortion laws. Or the Court could discard Roe, though it is considered unlikely, and return the matter entirely to the states.

MORE CRITICS

In 16 years, Roe has clearly lost adherents on the Court. The original two dissenters, Justices William H. Rehnquist and Byron R. White, could now be joined by Justice Sandra Day O'Connor, who has said that because of medical advances, the trimester approach is "on a collision course with itself." Justice Antonin Scalia is known to disapprove of Roe, and in all probability Justice Anthony M. Kennedy does, too — though that is not to say they are ready to overrule it.

In the Missouri case, the state argues that its statute is constitutional within the framework of Roe, and the law's opponents, half a dozen clinics and physicians, argue that it is not. On most points, the state lost in the lower Federal courts.

But the state's brief argues first that Roe is the wrong framework for a decision. The trimester rule, it says, "is inherently flawed because the point of viability is arbitrary and the state has a compelling interest in protecting life through all stages of pregnancy." Moreover, the state contends, the Court erred in identifying a "fundamental right" to abortion.

The law's challengers respond that there was strong historical basis for including abortion in the right to privacy and deciding that the state's interest is not compelling until the fetus is viable. Their brief also said: "In overruling Roe, the Court would, for the first time in its history, withdraw from constitutional protection a previously recognized fundamental personal liberty. Concomitantly, also in an unprecedented manner, constitutionally protected conduct undertaken daily by literally thousands of citizens would be open to abrupt criminalization."

The friend-of-the-court briefs expand on some of the arguments and present an array of new ones, conveying a sense of urgency at least as keen as the litigants'. Several of the briefs are excerpted below.

LAURA MANSNERUS

A DECISION WITHOUT A BASIS
The United States, as submitted by the Solicitor General's Office

Roe rests on assumptions that are not firmly grounded in the Constitution; it adopts an unworkable framework tying permissible state regulation of abortion to particular periods in pregnancy; and it has allowed courts to usurp the function of legislative bodies in weighing competing social, ethical and scientific factors in reaching a judgment as to how much state regulation is appropriate in this highly sensitive area. In similar circumstances, the Court has "not hesitated" to overrule a prior interpretation of the Constitution.

The Court's decision in Roe v. Wade rests upon two key premises — that there is a fundamental right to abortion and that the states do not have a compelling interest in protecting prenatal life throughout pregnancy. Neither premise, however, is supportable. The fundamental right to abortion can draw no support from the text of the Constitution or from history. ...

Roe's flaws are both illustrated and compounded by the manner in which the Court sought to implement its unfounded premises. The Court in Roe erected a framework for reviewing abortion regulations based on the division of pregnancy into three trimesters, with different types of state regulation permitted in each trimester. The dividing lines were grounded not in any principle of constitutional law, but rather in medical findings. As a consequence, the lines must either become increasingly arbitrary over time or change as medical technology changes. ...

We therefore believe that the time has come for the Court to abandon its efforts to impose a comprehensive solution to the abortion question. ... Other Western countries have, through the legislative process, reached reasonable accommodations of the competing interests involved in the abortion controversy. There is no reason to believe that American legislatures, if basic decision-making responsibility were returned to them, would not similarly arrive at humane solutions.

MOTHERHOOD WITHOUT CONSENT

The National Abortion Rights Action League, the Women's Legal Defense Fund and 75 other women's rights organizations

If this Court were to uphold abortion restrictions that force pregnant women to bear children, it would render empty the constitutional promise of liberty for women. ...

Forced motherhood threatens the core of a woman's constitutionally valued autonomy in two distinct ways.

First, state interference with abortion violates the principle of bodily integrity that underlies much of the 14th Amendment's promise of liberty. The process of bearing a child involves the most intimate and strenuous exercises of the female body and psyche; compelling a woman to devote her body, mind and soul to continue an unwanted pregnancy constitutes an invasion of our deepest sense of privacy and the primacy of self-determination. Forced continued pregnancy also entails a more tangible violation of physical liberty by subjecting women to a host of physical burdens and risks that range from prolonged discomfort and pain during pregnancy and delivery, to a substantial risk of specific medical complications, and even to death. ...

Second, state interference with abortion denies women the capacity to control their own lives in the most basic of ways. The bearing and raising of children places severe constraints on women's employment opportunities and therefore threatens their ability to support themselves and their families. ...

This Court cannot safely cede control over the availability of abortion to a political process that can be expected to undervalue both the importance to women of this aspect of their fundamental liberty and the burdens and risks of forced motherhood.

PROTECTION FOR EVERY PERSON

The Knights of Columbus

The present case is an appropriate vehicle for overruling Roe v. Wade even if the case could be decided under the Roe framework. ... As a practical matter, Roe's analytical framework is flawed beyond repair because it rests on "viability" — the point at which an unborn child can survive outside of the womb with artificial aid — to determine when a state may protect the life of "the developing young in the human uterus." As Justice O'Connor has pointed out, because viability is almost solely defined by ever-progressing technology, it is a constantly moving point that cannot be a neutral and stable basis for long-term constitutional adjudication.

More fundamentally, viability is an invalid benchmark for construing the meaning of "person" in the 14th Amendment because it has nothing to do with attributes of personhood, or a particularized state of being, but only the state of medical technology. Viability's true utility lies in its insight that a viable infant is certainly a person and that only limitations on technology prevent all unborn children from being viable. If a "viable" unborn child is a person, then so are all unborn children.

THE BURDEN OF MINORITIES
The National Council of Negro Women, the National Urban League and more than 100 other organizations

While women of all classes and colors will be endangered by any dismantling of the constitutional framework of Roe v. Wade, the burden will fall most heavily and inexorably on poor women, a vastly disproportionate number of whom are women of color — African-American, Latina, Native American and Asian. Women of color were overrepresented among the women who died, were left sterile or suffered other serious medical complications as a result of illegal abortions prior to this Court's decision in Roe v. Wade, and would be similarly affected by its reversal.

WHERE IS THIS RIGHT IN THE CONSTITUTION?
The Center for Judicial Studies and some members of Congress, including Senator Christopher S. Bond, Representative Henry J. Hyde and Senator Strom Thurmond

Roe v. Wade assumed or declared at various points that the Constitution guarantees a right to abortion, without ever identifying the basis of that right in a way that would guide its subsequent application. Although Roe v. Wade acknowledged that "the Constitution does not explicitly mention any right of privacy," it did not provide any specific reasons why the right to privacy included a right to abortion. Indeed, when one person demands access, free of governmental regulation, to a surgical procedure that is to be performed by another person — whether an abortion, a vasectomy, or a sex change operation — interference with the former's "privacy" is not an idea that comes readily to mind... .

From its inception, Roe v. Wade could not have been based on anything other than uniquely controversial moral judgments that the Constitution does not make. Making them calls for a competence and democratic legitimacy that Federal courts lack by design. As a result, it is not surprising that Roe v. Wade's 16-year journey through our system of justice has left a trail of unprincipled decisions and legislative confusion, which, unless ended, bode more of the same for the future.

DECISIONS FOR DOCTORS AND PATIENTS
The American Medical Association and other medical organizations

The essence of the liberty interest denominated as the right to privacy is the concept that an individual in certain circumstances has a right to be let alone, and that the individual must thus have "independence in making certain kinds of important decisions." As this Court has recognized, that right encompasses matters concerning marriage and procreation. The specter of governmental agents unnecessarily interfering with such private, individual decisions is antithetical to basic concepts of individual liberty in a free society.

Moreover, and of particular significance to amici and their members, the right to privacy which is derived from the concept of liberty also encompasses the right of an individual to make decisions about his or her medical care and treatment. As our discussion of the health implications of pregnancy and abortion makes clear, the Court's assumptions about the importance of this particular medical treatment decision are as true today as they were in 1973.

WHERE SCIENCE HAS STOPPED

167 scientists and physicians, including 11 Nobel laureates

There is no scientific consensus that a human life begins at conception, at a given stage of fetal development, or at birth. The question of "when a human life begins" cannot be answered by reference to scientific principles like those with which we predict planetary movement. The answer to that question will depend on each individual's social, religious, philosophical, ethical and moral beliefs and values.

Science can, however, provide answers to certain concrete questions regarding prenatal development that have arisen in the controversy over abortion and Roe v. Wade. For example, several amici assert that medical advances are undermining Roe v. Wade by moving the point of fetal viability briskly and inexorably toward the date of conception. Science is capable of addressing — and in this case refuting — such arguments.

The earliest point of viability has remained virtually unchanged at approximately 24 weeks of gestation since 1973, and there is no reason to believe that a change is either imminent or inevitable. The reason that viability has not been pushed significantly back toward the point of conception is that critical organs, particularly lungs and kidneys, do not mature before that time. Progress in science, therefore, has not made obsolete the trimester framework based on viability articulated in Roe v. Wade.

OVERREACHING BY THE COURTS

127 members of the Missouri General Assembly

For over 150 years, the State of Missouri has consistently expressed its opposition to abortion on demand. The legislature and courts of Missouri, moreover, have extended the protection of state laws to "all humans, born and unborn," in contexts ranging from abortion regulation to criminal law and property law. These regulatory efforts all permissibly express the state's compelling interest in the protection of unborn life. ...

By invalidating the regulations at issue here, the lower courts improperly intruded upon the legislative arena. Basic prudential and constitutional concerns — including the principle of popular sovereignty, the inherent limitations of the judicial process and the need to preserve public confidence in the judiciary — counsel substantial deference to legislative resolutions of controversial issues of public policy.

THE RISKS THAT WOMEN TOOK
2,887 women who have had abortions

Prior to Roe v. Wade, this country was in the midst of a medical, social and legal crisis caused by the illegality of abortion. Despite the fact that abortion was illegal or highly restricted in its availability throughout the United States before Roe v. Wade, women did have abortions, for compelling reasons. The numbers of illegally induced abortions in the United States in the 1960's ranged up to estimates of 1.5 million a year. Women risked their lives and health in order to meet their inevitable need for abortion. ...

A large number of illegal abortions were self-induced or performed by unskilled and untrained personnel working under dangerous septic conditions, unaccountable to professional guidelines and safeguards and unreached by ordinary government licensing procedures or other safeguards.

Foes of Abortion Prepare Measures for State Action

BY E. J. DIONNE JR. | **JULY 5, 1989**

The plan is to include new bills and others once thought to be unconstitutional.

WASHINGTON, JULY 4 — Opponents of abortion, moving to take advantage of the Supreme Court ruling Monday, are preparing measures for state legislatures around the nation that would increase restrictions on abortion.

Burke Balch, state legislative coordinator for the National Right to Life Committee, said these would include new measures as well as proposals that were introduced in previous years but that were regarded as unconstitutional before the Court's ruling.

Among them are a prohibition on abortions in cases in which a couple wants a child of the other sex, and a way for the father to prevent a woman from having an abortion. Mr. Balch said the movement would also seek more stringent curbs on the ability of minors to have abortions, notably by requiring parental consent.

DELAYS ON STATE LEVEL

Mr. Balch and other opponents of abortion conceded today that most states will probably postpone action on abortion legislation until this fall or next year, since almost all the nation's state legislatures have gone home and are unlikely to return for special sessions.

In the meantime, Kate Michelman, executive director of the National Abortion Rights Action League, said her group was considering bringing suits in state courts to defend the right to choose abortion. Its hope is that at least some state courts will find that the right to choose abortion is inherent in state constitutions.

The Supreme Court has no jurisdiction to hear appeals in cases that have been decided entirely on the basis of a state constitution, except in instances where federally guaranteed constitutional rights are abridged. Ms. Michelman said state rulings in favor of abortion rights would keep abortion legal in some places even if the Supreme Court later overturned Roe v. Wade, the 1973 ruling that legalized abortion.

DECISION ON MISSOURI LAW

The actions were prompted by the Court's 5-to-4 decision Monday upholding a Missouri law that restricted public employees from performing abortions and barred the use of public buildings for the procedure. The law also requires doctors to perform tests to determine if the fetus is viable if they believe a woman seeking an abortion is at least 20 weeks pregnant.

The effect of the ruling is to give states the right to impose sharp new restrictions on abortion.

Partisans on both sides of the issue said that quick action on abortion was possible in only about a dozen states where legislatures are in session or might be called into session to act on anti-abortion bills, and would probably occur in fewer than half of them.

"Most of the legislatures that are still in session are ones that probably won't do anything," said Nancy Broff, political and legislative director for the National Abortion Rights Action League, which favors keeping abortion legal.

ANTI-ABORTION MEASURES

Still, in the aftermath of the decision Monday, matters are moving quickly in some states. In Pennsylvania, State Representative Stephen F. Freind, a Republican, said he would push for a series of anti-abortion measures for the Legislature's fall session. In New Jersey, Speaker Chuck Hardwick said he would convene a special meeting of the Assembly this fall to debate abortion.

Mr. Balch said that one of the anti-abortion movement's central goals is to condition a woman's right to an abortion on her reasons for having it. He acknowledged the difficulty of establishing motivation.

But he said that in the absence of an outright ban on abortion, requiring women to state reasons for having abortions would reduce the number of abortions.

Looking toward 1990 and beyond, the abortion rights league estimates that anti-abortion forces are strongest in nine states: Pennsylvania, Georgia, Alabama, Louisiana, Oklahoma, Missouri, Minnesota, Nebraska and Utah. The two sides generally agree that the states least likely to approve abortion restrictions are Washington, Colorado, New Mexico, North Carolina, New York, Connecticut and Maine.

As the partisans planned strategy, the decision's political effect was felt immediately in New York City and New Jersey, where people will be voting this fall.

In New York City, Mayor Edward I. Koch accused Rudolph Giuliani, a Republican candidate for Mayor, of trying to sidestep the matter by declaring that abortion is not a city issue. In New Jersey, Representative James J. Florio, the Democratic candidate for Governor, affirmed his support for abortion rights, while Representative Jim Courter, the Republican candidate, said he generally supported the latest Supreme Court decision.

State officials around the nation reacted to the decision with a mixture of militancy, confusion and fear.

Staunch opponents of abortion said they were eager to pass new restrictions as soon as feasible. Terry Abbott, a spokesman for Gov. Guy Hunt, said the Alabama Governor "will pursue any legal means possible to restrict abortion as much as possible."

Brian Ballard, director of operations for Gov. Bob Martinez of Florida, describing the state as "pro life," predicted that the Governor would call a special session of the Legislature in "early fall to make abortion on demand more restrictive."

Advocates of abortion rights were just as quick to pledge opposition to any new regulations. Gov. John McKernan of Maine, a Republican, said, "I intend to oppose any legislative attempts to have state government play a wider role in regulating a woman's right to make a choice on abortion in the first two trimesters of pregnancy." Gov. Gerald L. Baliles of Virginia, a Democrat, said: "My view is that medical care should be available to a woman who wants to determine whether to continue her pregnancy and that decision should be hers to make, however she chooses to make it."

UNEASE WITH NEW AUTHORITY

Many state politicians echoed Roger D. McKellips, the South Dakota State Senate minority leader, in expressing unease with the new authority the ruling had thrust upon states.

"It's going be a mess," Mr. McKellips said. "It's going to cause some terribly emotional debates, irrational debates, illogical debates, it's going to cause some problems." He predicted anti-abortion legislators "are going to go as absolutely as far as they can."

Gov. James R. Thompson of Illinois, a Republican, urged caution. "I think we ought to take the summer and seriously consider this," he said. "Illinois might set a model for the nation by engaging in reasoned discussion and hearings."

As the abortion battle moves to the states, here is the outlook in states that are expected to be major battlegrounds. In other states, prospects for immediate change seem less likely:

Northeast

New York was one of the states to legalize abortion before the Roe v. Wade decision and one of the few where the state finances Medicaid abortions. "New York state was a landmark state in this movement and any regression by New York would certainly be of national significance," said Assemblyman Richard Gottfried, a Manhattan Democrat.

Gov. Mario M. Cuomo has long said that while he personally opposes abortion, he believes himself bound to uphold Roe v. Wade. But now that the Court seems to be backing away from Roe, Mr. Cuomo will be pressed to clarify his stand.

In New Jersey, the abortion issue will probably be settled at the polls in the race between Mr. Florio and Mr. Courter. Both sides rate Connecticut as unlikely to approve new abortion restrictions, while Pennsylvania is rated as likely to enact restrictions as early as this fall.

Middle West

Missouri, Minnesota and Nebraska are generally rated as among the most firmly anti-abortion states in the nation. Kansas leans against abortion, but Gov. Mike Hayden, a Republican, has not taken a clear stance.

In Iowa, the abortion issue is expected to play a major role in the 1990 Senate race between Senator Tom Harkin, a Democrat who supports abortion rights, and Representative Tom Tauke, a Republican who opposes abortion. Gov. Terry E. Branstad of Iowa, a Republican, is opposed to abortion and said he was "pleased to hear that the Missouri statute was upheld."

In Michigan, Gov. James E. Blanchard firmly favors abortion rights and said he would veto restrictive legislation. Right-to-life advocates see a good chance for anti-abortion legislation in South Dakota and Kentucky, while Indiana, Illinois and Ohio are seen as potential battlegrounds.

South

North Carolina is the Southern state least likely to restrict abortion, while Louisiana, Alabama and Georgia seem most likely to do so.

Florida will be a major battleground, especially if Governor Martinez calls a special session of the Legislature. Anti-abortion forces say the outlook for them is good there and in Mississippi. In Arkansas, the issue could severely test Gov. Bill Clinton, a liberal with Presidential hopes. Gov. Carroll Campbell of South Carolina, a Republican, said he had asked the state's Attorney General and key legislative leaders to work toward introducing legislation reflecting the decision when the next session begins in January 1990.

In Virginia, a decision is likely to await the results of this year's gubernatorial election. Texas may hold a special legislative session.

The West

The region seems, on balance, in favor of abortion rights. Abortion rights advocates seem especially strong in Washington, Colorado, New Mexico, Oregon, Alaska and Hawaii. Utah seems especially likely to restrict abortion, and the anti-abortion movement believes it is strong in Wyoming and Idaho.

California will be a battleground, but action seems unlikely until next year and is likely to focus on court-mandated public financing of abortions. The state's flexible referendum law could put the issue on the ballot.

High Court, 5-4, Affirms Right to Abortion But Allows Most of Pennsylvania's Limits

BY LINDA GREENHOUSE | JUNE 30, 1992

WASHINGTON, JUNE 29 — By the narrowest of margins, and in words reflecting anger and anguish alike at its continuing role in the center of the storm over abortion, the Supreme Court today reaffirmed what it called the "essence" of the constitutional right to abortion while at the same time permitting some new state restrictions.

The 5-to-4 ruling redefined and limited the abortion right to some degree. But it left it stronger than many abortion-rights supporters had expected and opponents had hoped for from a Court that had appeared for the last three years to be on a course leading inevitably to the evisceration, if not complete overruling, of Roe v. Wade, the 1973 decision that established abortion as a fundamental right.

UNCONSTITUTIONAL PROHIBITIONS

While the ruling upheld part of a Pennsylvania law regulating access to abortions, the majority left no doubt that laws prohibiting all or most abortions are unconstitutional. Louisiana, Utah and Guam have passed such laws and other states have been considering them.

In the opinion for the Court, unusual for being written jointly by Justices Sandra Day O'Connor, Anthony M. Kennedy and David H. Souter, and joined in part by Justices Harry A. Blackmun and John Paul Stevens, the majority said that Roe v. Wade established a "rule of law and a component of liberty we cannot renounce."

The majority said the 1973 decision had acquired a "rare precedential force" and could be overturned "under fire" only "at the cost of both profound and unnecessary damage to the Court's legitimacy, and to the nation's commitment to the rule of law."

There was little doubt that the "under fire" comment was aimed, at least in part, at the White House, both under President Bush and his predecessor, Ronald Reagan. In the first paragraph of its 60-page opinion, the majority noted pointedly that "the United States, as it has done in five other cases in the last decade, again asks us to overrule Roe."

A NEW ANALYSIS

The decision upheld parts of Pennsylvania's Abortion Control Act and struck down another part, applying for the first time a new analysis that asks whether a state abortion regulation has the purpose or effect of imposing an "undue burden." This was defined as a "substantial obstacle in the path of a woman seeking an abortion before the fetus attains viability."

Under this analysis, the Court said that four sections of Pennsylvania's law did not impose an undue burden on the right to abortion and were constitutional. These sections require a woman to delay an abortion for 24 hours after listening to a presentation at the medical office intended to persuade them to change her mind; require teen-agers to have the consent of one parent or a judge; specify the medical emergencies in which the other requirements will be waived, and require the doctor or clinic to make statistical reports to the state. At the same time, by a 5-4 vote, the Court struck down a fifth provision requiring a married woman to tell her husband of her intent to have an abortion.

Gov. Robert P. Casey of Pennsylvania, a Democrat whose opposition to abortion has made him something of a pariah in his party, said the Court's analysis vindicated his state's approach to regulating abortion. "Today's decision upholding the Pennsylvania law is a victory for the unborn child, the most powerless member of the human family," he said.

Abortion-rights supporters said the ruling would encourage more state restrictions and that the waiting period, in particular, would make abortions more difficult and expensive for women who would have to make two trips to abortion clinics that might be hundreds of miles from their homes.

Seven Justices supported these requirements. In addition to Justices O'Connor, Kennedy and Souter, they were Chief Justice William H. Rehnquist and Justices Antonin Scalia, Byron R. White and Clarence Thomas. These four Justices said that the Court should not only have upheld these regulations, but should also have overturned Roe v. Wade itself.

Justices Blackmun and Stevens, in separate opinions of their own, said that four provisions should be held unconstitutional. And they joined the O'Connor-Kennedy-Souter group to strike down the husband-notification provision.

This provision contained several exceptions, including one for women who believed their husbands would physically injure them on learning of a planned abortion.

But the Court said that this did not sufficiently protect women who face psychological as well as physical abuse and who may have "very good reasons for not wishing to inform their husbands of their decision to obtain an abortion."

The Court added, "A state may not give to a man the kind of dominion over his wife that parents exercise over their children."

SCATHING DISSENTS

In dissenting opinions, Chief Justice Rehnquist and Justice Scalia offered scathing critiques of the Court's opinion. Each signed the other's opinion, and both opinions were also signed by Justices White and Thomas. The overlap was somewhat puzzling, because the two opinions expressed very different, even contradictory, views about what the majority had accomplished.

Chief Justice Rehnquist said the Court had not actually reaffirmed Roe v. Wade, but had rendered it a "facade," replacing its framework with a standard "created largely out of whole cloth" and "not built to last."

"Roe v. Wade stands as a sort of judicial Potemkin village," the Chief Justice said, "which may be pointed out to passersby as a monument to the importance of adhering to precedent."

Justice Scalia, on the other hand, declared that "the imperial judiciary lives," and appeared to concede to the majority its assertion that abortion remained on a solid constitutional foundation, although one he strongly disagreed with.

"By foreclosing all democratic outlet for the deep passions this issue arouse," Justice Scalia said, "by banishing the issue from the political forum that gives all participants, even the losers, the satisfaction of a fair hearing and an honest fight, by continuing the imposition of a rigid national rule instead of allowing for regional differences, the Court merely prolongs and intensifies the anguish."

The case, Planned Parenthood v. Casey, No. 91-744, gave the two newest Justices their first opportunity to rule in an abortion case. Both Bush nominees — Justice Souter, who joined the Court in 1990, and Justice Thomas, who told the Senate Judiciary Committee last September that he had never discussed Roe v. Wade — had been careful to avoid giving their views on abortion during their confirmation hearings.

SURPRISE FROM 2 JUSTICES

The real surprise in the decision, however, lay not in their votes but in the votes of two Justices chosen by Ronald Reagan, Justices O'Connor and Kennedy, who in previous opinions were sharp critics of Roe v. Wade.

Just three years ago, when the Court upheld portions of a restrictive Missouri abortion law in Webster v. Reproductive Health Services, Justice Kennedy joined a plurality opinion by Chief Justice Rehnquist that would have essentially overturned Roe v. Wade and replaced it with the lowest level of constitutional protection. Justice O'Connor was a consistent dissenter during her early years on the Court.

In her first abortion opinion in 1983, she was sharply critical of the precedent, declaring that it had established a doctrine "at war with itself" because the date of fetal viability was, she said, moving ever earlier toward the first months of pregnancy. In her early opinions, Justice O'Connor proposed replacing Roe v. Wade with an "undue burden" test that would have allowed more restrictions than the test she, Justice Kennedy and Justice Souter adopted today. Because she had initially referred to the state's interest in the life of the fetus as "compelling," it had not been clear whether her original "undue burden" test would find it unconstitutional for a state to ban abortion.

Today's opinion made no reference to a "compelling" state interest in fetal life and acknowledged that some of her previous statements had been "inconsistent." "We answer the question, left open in previous opinions discussing the undue burden formulation, whether a law designed to further the state's interest in fetal life which imposes an undue burden on the woman's decision before fetal viability could be constitutional," the three Justices wrote. "The answer is no."

The important difference between today's decision and Roe v. Wade lay in the standard of review by which courts are to evaluate abortion restrictions. As the Court had interpreted Roe v. Wade until the Webster decision three years ago, abortion was a "fundamental" right that could not be restricted except to serve a "compelling" state interest, a standard of review known as "strict scrutiny" under which nearly all restrictions on abortion during the first two trimesters of pregnancy were found invalid.

But the new "undue burden" standard will permit considerably more regulation during that period. The Court today overruled two decisions, one from 1983 and the other from 1986, that had struck down, applying strict scrutiny analysis, 24-hour waiting periods and informed consent provisions much like the ones the Court upheld today. The decision today upheld a ruling last fall by the United States Court of Appeals for the Third Circuit, in Philadelphia.

MORE WRANGLING AHEAD

The decision today was certainly not the Court's final word on the abortion issue, and it may not even be the final word on the Pennsylvania law. The majority indicated that because the law had not yet taken effect, and because the abortion clinics that challenged the law had not had occasion to document the effects of the waiting period and other provisions, the Court's door would be open to the argument that provisions that did not appear to impose an "undue burden" in theory might do so in fact.

Justice Blackmun, in his separate opinion, said he was "pleased" that the Court was open to reconsidering its conclusion and "confident" that the evidence would prove the clinics' case.

The opinion of Justice Blackmun, the author of Roe v. Wade, took an extraordinarily personal tone, reflecting relief that the Court had not flatly overturned Roe v. Wade as he had publicly predicted, and disappointment that his legacy still remained under attack.

In a bitter dissenting opinion in the Webster case three years ago, he warned that darkness was approaching and "a chill wind blows." Today, he said, "But now, just when so many expected the darkness to fall, the flame has grown bright." He commended Justices O'Connor, Souter and Kennedy for "an act of personal courage and constitutional principle."

But he warned that Roe v. Wade was only one vote away from being completely overruled. "I am 83 years old," he said. "I cannot remain on this Court forever." He predicted a fierce confirmation battle over the nomination of a successor. Justice Blackmun, the oldest member of the Court, has said within the past few days that he is not planning to retire at this point.

Given the Justices' personal feelings, the scene in the courtroom this morning, on the last day of the Court's term, was one of drama. Justice O'Connor read a section of the joint opinion, stressing that abortion was a difficult personal issue for the members of the Court. But she said, "Our obligation is to define the liberty of all, not to mandate our own moral code."

Ruling Allows Major Center
Its First Clinic for Abortions

BY THE NEW YORK TIMES | FEB. 15, 1998

CHICAGO, FEB. 14 — A Federal judge's ruling could allow Planned Parenthood to open an abortion clinic in Bettendorf, Iowa, in the nation's largest metropolitan area without such services.

The ruling on Thursday by Judge Charles R. Wolle of United States District Court in Des Moines said that Bettendorf, one of the Quad Cities on the Iowa-Illinois border, was using its zoning ordinances unfairly to prohibit Planned Parenthood from developing the clinic.

Judge Wolle said the city applied its laws specifically to prevent the clinic from being developed, "violating the constitutional rights of the women who would be served" in the area, which includes Davenport, Iowa, and Moline and Rock Island, Ill.

The area has a well-financed, well-organized presence of abortion opponents, but Greg Jager, the Bettendorf City Attorney, said the city was not singling out Planned Parenthood.

"Forty percent of this city is zoned for commercial use," Mr. Jager said. "Planned Parenthood could have chosen to build their clinic anywhere in that area without a problem." He said the area the organization chose was near residential property where many people opposed the clinic.

Connie Cook, the regional director for Planned Parenthood in eastern Iowa, said her organization looked throughout the Quad Cities area and determined that the Bettendorf location was the only one that matched the group's needs.

"We looked and looked and looked," Ms. Cook said. "We needed a large site that is easily accessible, yet somewhat secluded, to best serve the needs of the women in this area."

"My experience is that no matter where we would have looked, the city would have fought us," she said.

The Quad Cities have a population of 320,000, but the nearest clinic is 50 miles away, in Iowa City. Ms. Cook said Planned Parenthood would continue with its development plans and hoped to break ground for the clinic in May and be in operation by the fall.

Abortion opponents, however, have vowed to continue fighting the clinic. Launa Stoltenberg, a spokeswoman for the Life and Family Coalition, told The Associated Press, "My faith says we're not going to see a clinic there."

The city is also considering its options. Mr. Jager said the executive committee of the City Council would meet on Tuesday to consider an appeal or other action.

The 2.3-acre site for the clinic is in an area that is not zoned for commercial use. Planned Parenthood petitioned the city to change the zoning, and despite a recommendation by the planning and zoning commission, the City Council denied the request. The judge's order converts the disputed land to commercial property.

Ms. Cook said that support for Planned Parenthood in the area had been overwhelming.

"Our opponents are very organized and loud, but they do not speak for all of the citizens here," she said.

"We have been working very hard to build relationships in the community and expressed our desire to work cooperatively. We have done everything we can to be good neighbors."

Opponents of Abortions Cheer New Administration

BY ROBIN TONER | JAN. 23, 2001

WASHINGTON, JAN. 22 — Jubilant over the prospect of a friend in the White House changing abortion policy, opponents of legalized abortion rallied in the nation's capital today on the 28th anniversary of Roe v. Wade, the Supreme Court decision that declared a constitutional right to abortion.

"We share a great goal: to work toward a day when every child is welcomed in life and protected in law," Mr. Bush declared in a statement read by Representative Christopher H. Smith, Republican of New Jersey, to a sprawling crowd beneath the Washington Monument. "We know that this will not come easily or all at once, but the goal leads us onward, to build a culture of life, affirming that every person and every stage and season of life, is created equally in God's image."

In a move fraught with symbolism, Mr. Bush announced that he would reimpose a ban on federal aid to international organizations that perform or "actively promote abortion as a method of family planning." He was thus reversing an action taken by Mr. Clinton exactly eight years before, also on the anniversary of Roe v. Wade, underscoring the fact that in the deeply polarized struggle over abortion, one side had won, the other lost.

Family planning and reproductive rights organizations denounced the president's action as a return to "the global gag rule" of the former Bush and Reagan eras, an effort to deny fundamental freedoms of speech and political action to those providing health care abroad. It is "a restriction that would be unconstitutional if imposed here in the U.S.," in the words of Kate Michelman, president of the National Abortion and Reproductive Rights Action League.

But the crowd at the "March for Life," an annual ritual here, roared in approval when Senator Sam Brownback, Republican of Kansas, announced the White House move.

Anti-abortion activists shout slogans as they protest outside the U.S. Supreme Court Jan. 22, 2001 after a march in Washington.

For all the good spirit in the anti-abortion ranks, there were signs of concern after 10 days of conflicting signals from the Bush team. Some here were clearly rankled by the testimony of John Ashcroft, the nominee for attorney general, before the Senate Judiciary Committee last week that Roe v. Wade was "settled law" and thus the administration would not seek opportunities to challenge it. The decision will never be "settled law" in America because it is so profoundly wrong, declared a leader of the march, Nellie Gray.

Miss Gray also served notice that abortion opponents would not be satisfied with incremental victories. "What we're saying to all Washington officialdom is this — it's on your watch now," she said. "Tax cuts are important, but they're not the top priority." The top priority must be the abortion issue, she argued.

The first lady, Laura Bush, also clearly caused some concern when she said last week that she did not believe the Roe v. Wade decision should be overturned. Representative Smith, a longtime abortion foe, said in an interview that Mrs. Bush's comments came as "a bit of a surprise" but that he was confident in Mr. Bush's "faithfulness" to his anti-abortion convictions. Mr. Bush himself, in an interview with NBC today, said "I've always said that Roe v. Wade was a judicial reach."

One speaker after another today celebrated the departure of Mr. Clinton, a close ally of the abortion rights movement.

"The long eight years is over," declared former Representative Robert K. Dornan, Republican of California. "We have a man of deep faith in the White House, and we will have a man of deep faith as the nation's top cop."

Representative Steve Chabot, Republican of Ohio, declared, "Boy, it sounds good to say 'former President Clinton.' "

Organizers said they were delighted by the healthy size of the crowd this year, but the United States Park Police no longer provides crowd estimates for marches and demonstrations. Buses came from Allentown, Pa., St. Louis and points beyond and between, many of them from Catholic schools and parishes. And there was an array of Catholic church leaders on the stage.

Bishop William G. Curlin of Charlotte, N.C., said as he marched up the muddy Washington Mall, "It will take time to change hearts." But Bishop Curlin added of Mr. Bush, "He gives us hope. That's what's important today. You felt under the former administration that there was no hope as far as the sanctity of life issue."

Managing those expectations, now that Mr. Bush is no longer candidate but president, may be the challenge. During the campaign, Mr. Bush embraced a Republican platform that called for a ban on abortions, which won him the loyalty of the party's strong anti-abortion base. But he rarely campaigned on the issue, and when pressed said he thought such a ban was a distant goal.

But the abortion opponents now clearly expect quick action on issues like a review of the abortion pill RU-486 and a ban on the late-term procedure that opponents call partial birth abortion.

"As long as Roe v. Wade is the law of the land, Jan. 22 will live in infamy," said Wanda Franz, president of the National Right to Life Committee. "It is no exaggeration to say that the court's action in Roe v. Wade prepared the path for what is now rightfully called the 'culture of death.' It is also fair to say that Roe v. Wade and the subsequent decisions based on and extending Roe v. Wade are the most radical decisions in the history of the Supreme Court."

Bush Rule Makes Fetuses Eligible for Health Benefits

BY ROBERT PEAR | SEPT. 28, 2002

WASHINGTON, SEPT. 27 — The Bush administration issued final rules today allowing states to define a fetus as a child eligible for government-subsidized health care under the Children's Health Insurance Program.

" 'Child' means an individual under the age of 19, including the period from conception to birth," the regulation says.

Tommy G. Thompson, the secretary of health and human services, said the rule would increase the number of low-income women who receive prenatal care. "What better way to allow kids to have the best start in life, a healthy start?" Mr. Thompson asked.

But critics said the change was a backdoor effort to advance the administration's anti-abortion agenda and to establish a legal precedent for recognizing the fetus as a person.

Under the rule, states can use federal money to provide prenatal care to low-income pregnant women, even those who are illegal immigrants and would otherwise be ineligible.

"It does not make sense to try to impute an immigration status to an unborn child based on the status of the mother," the administration said. Under the Constitution, a person born in this country is a United States citizen, even if the mother is an illegal immigrant. So the child may qualify for coverage at birth.

The administration said the rule would increase insurance coverage for prenatal care and delivery. "This is compassionate conservatism at its best," Mr. Thompson said.

But Senator Jon Corzine, Democrat of New Jersey, said the administration was making "an outrageous attempt to politicize prenatal care, something that should be dealt with in a simple, straightforward way."

Laurie Rubiner, vice president of the National Partnership for Women and Families, an advocacy group that supports abortion rights, said the rule was "a cynical move by the administration to court Latinos and anti-abortion groups at the same time." The administration, Ms. Rubiner said, has opposed Congressional efforts to restore health benefits to tens of thousands of low-income immigrants who have not become citizens and lost coverage as a result of the 1996 welfare law.

Gloria Feldt, president of the Planned Parenthood Federation of America, said: "This regulation is ridiculous. It elevates the status of the fetus above that of the woman. It does not provide prenatal care to the woman in whose body the fetus resides. It makes the fetus eligible for prenatal care, but treats the woman as a mere vessel, an incubator."

The Bush administration said federal money from the Children's Health Insurance Program could not be used to provide postpartum services or follow-up care to a woman after delivery, unless the woman herself was younger than 19.

The National Right to Life Committee praised the new rule. "Many unborn children, and their mothers as well, are now eligible to receive proper prenatal care as part of the children's health program," said Douglas D. Johnson, legislative director of the committee.

Mr. Thompson insisted that he was not trying to placate opponents of abortion. "This, to me, is not an abortion issue," Mr. Thompson said. "It's strictly a health issue. Our goal is simply to promote the health of that unborn baby. That's my motivation."

The administration estimated that the new rule would increase federal spending by $330 million over five years. For the purpose of calculating costs, it predicted that 13 states would choose to cover "unborn children" and that 30,000 fetuses would gain coverage as a result.

"The health status of children will improve to the extent that their mothers receive prenatal care," it said.

Critics said the administration was trying to create a precedent for viewing a fetus as a separate physical and legal entity, with its own rights. By enhancing the status of the fetus, they said, the administration undercuts a woman's right to control her life and to obtain an abortion.

But the administration said the rule would not set up "an adversarial relationship between the mother and her unborn child." Moreover, it said, "there is no conflict, as the services to be provided benefit both mother and child."

When the Supreme Court recognized a right to abortion in Roe v. Wade, in 1973, it said that the word "person," as used in the 14th Amendment to the Constitution, "does not include the unborn." The Bush administration said it saw no contradiction between that ruling and the new rule, which gives states "maximum flexibility" to include a fetus among those eligible for the child health program.

Ruling Opens New Arena in the Debate on Abortion

BY ADAM LIPTAK | OCT. 16, 2002

A PREGNANT WOMAN may use deadly force to protect her fetus even when she does not fear for her own life, the Michigan Court of Appeals has ruled. Legal experts say the decision has opened another front in the legal wars surrounding abortion.

The court emphasized that its decision was a narrow one, concerning only assaults against pregnant women, but it acknowledged that it was entering charged legal terrain.

"We are obviously aware of the raging debate occurring in this country regarding the point at which a fetus becomes a person entitled to all the protections of the state and federal constitutions," Judge Patrick M. Meter wrote for a unanimous three-judge panel.

The case arose from a lovers' quarrel involving Jaclyn Kurr and her boyfriend, Antonio Pena, the man who had impregnated her. She later testified that after Mr. Pena punched her in the stomach, she responded by stabbing him in the chest with a kitchen knife, killing him. At the time she was 16 to 17 weeks pregnant.

She was charged with manslaughter, and the jury rejected her assertion that she had been acting in self-defense. She was sentenced to 5 to 20 years in prison.

This month, the appeals court reversed her conviction and ordered a new trial. It said the trial judge should have let her argue that she was defending not only herself but also "her unborn children."

The court noted that the age of Ms. Kurr's fetuses — she was apparently carrying quadruplets — meant that they could not have survived outside the womb and that she could abort them under the Supreme Court's decision in Roe v. Wade. She miscarried a few weeks later.

"One is left with a most peculiar legal situation," said John C. Mayoue, an Atlanta lawyer who is an expert in the various ways the law treats embryos and fetuses. "Although she may use deadly force to protect the viable or nonviable fetus, thereby ending someone's life, she also has the constitutional right to terminate the pregnancy herself without consequence."

Linda Rosenthal, a lawyer with the Center for Reproductive Law and Policy, said the decision was consistent with the Supreme Court's abortion jurisprudence.

"When a woman is carrying a wanted pregnancy and she has made that decision, which is constitutionally protected, she has the right to protect the embryo or fetus," she said.

About half the states have laws making assaults that cause miscarriages or stillbirths criminal. In debates in Congress last year about a possible federal version of the law, opponents understood the central issue to be abortion and not crime.

"We should have no illusions about the purposes of this bill," said Representative Jerrold L. Nadler, Democrat of New York, about the Unborn Victims of Violence Act. "It is another battle in the war of symbols in the abortion debate, in which opponents of a woman's right to choose attempt to portray fetuses, from the earliest moments of development, as children."

He continued: "If causing a miscarriage is murder, then, by implication, so is abortion, the Supreme Court never mind."

Michigan law allows people to use deadly force to defend themselves when they believe their lives are in danger or when they feel threatened by serious bodily harm. Ms. Kurr failed to persuade the jury that the punches amounted to either.

The law there allows the use of deadly force in defense of others. The trial judge ruled that the fetuses Ms. Kurr was carrying were not "others" for these purposes.

"I believe in order to be able to assert a defense of others there has to be a living human being existing independent of your client," Judge Richard Lyon Lamb of the Kalamazoo County Circuit Court, said to Ms. Kurr's lawyer. "Under 22 weeks, there are no others."

In reversing the conviction, the appeals court held that the concept of defending others "should also extend to the protection of a fetus, viable or nonviable, from an assault against the mother."

The court stressed that it recognized the defense only in the context of an assault, thus excluding the destruction of embryos existing outside the body and medical abortions.

Gail Rodwan, Ms. Kurr's lawyer, said the opinion was limited in its holding but not in its implications.

"The opinion certainly does recognize the sense that the fetus was another separate from the mother," she said. "That may be something people could seize on."

Anti-abortion advocates have on occasion asserted the defense of others to charges like criminal trespass in blocking access to abortion clinics. In that context, the defense has been rejected.

Through her lawyer, Ms. Kurr, who remains in prison, declined to comment.

Ms. Rodwan, in her brief on behalf of Ms. Kurr, said that abortion rights should not be affected by a ruling in her client's favor. "Abortion providers act under protection of the law," she wrote. "Antonio Pena, with his assaultive conduct, did not."

Heather Bergmann, a prosecutor, said the state would ask the Michigan Supreme Court to hear the case. Its principal argument, she said, will be that the right to self-defense is adequate to protect both pregnant women and their fetuses.

Ms. Bergmann mentioned that she herself had never been pregnant. "I would guess that as soon as I did become pregnant," she said, "I would think I would be very concerned if someone came after my stomach."

In Support of Abortion, It's Personal vs. Political

BY SHERYL GAY STOLBERG | NOV. 28, 2009

WASHINGTON — In the early 1950s, a coal miner's daughter from rural Kentucky named Louise McIntosh encountered the shadowy world of illegal abortion. A friend was pregnant, with no prospects for marriage, and Ms. McIntosh was keeper of a secret that, if spilled, could have led to family disgrace. The turmoil ended quietly in a doctor's office, and the friend went on to marry and have four children.

Today, Louise McIntosh is Representative Louise M. Slaughter, Democrat of New York. At 80, she is co-chairwoman of the Congressional Pro-Choice Caucus — a member of what Nancy Keenan, president of Naral Pro-Choice America, calls "the menopausal militia."

The militia was working overtime in Washington last week, plotting strategy for the coming debate over President Obama's proposed health care overhaul. With the Senate set to take up its measure on Monday, a fight over federal funding for abortion is threatening to thwart the bill — a development that has both galvanized the abortion rights movement and forced its leaders to turn inward, raising questions about how to carry their agenda forward in a complex, 21st-century world.

It has been nearly 37 years since Roe v. Wade, the landmark Supreme Court decision that established a right to abortion, and in that time, an entire generation — including Mr. Obama, who was 11 when Roe was decided — has grown up without memories like those Ms. Slaughter says are "seared into my mind." The result is a generational divide — not because younger women are any less supportive of abortion rights than their elders, but because their frame of reference is different.

"Here is a generation that has never known a time when abortion has been illegal," said Anna Greenberg, a Democratic pollster who studies attitudes toward abortion. "For many of them, the daily experience is: It's legal and if you really need one you can probably figure out how to get one. So when we send out e-mail alerts saying, 'Oh my God, write to your senator,' it's hard for young people to have that same sense of urgency."

Polls over the last two decades have shown that a clear majority of Americans support the right to abortion, and there's little evidence of a difference between those over 30 and under 30, but the vocabulary of the debate has shifted with the political culture. Ms. Keenan, who is 57, says women like her, who came of age when abortion was illegal, tend to view it in stark political terms — as a right to be defended, like freedom of speech or freedom of religion. But younger people tend to view abortion as a personal issue, and their interests are different.

The 30- to 40-somethings — "middle-school moms and dads," Ms. Keenan calls them — are more concerned with educating their children about sex, and generally too busy to be bothered with political causes. The 25-and-under crowd, animated by activism, sees a deeper threat in climate change or banning gay marriage or the Darfur genocide than in any rollback of reproductive rights. Naral is running focus groups with these "millennials" to better learn how they think.

"The language and values, if you are older, is around the right to control your own body, reproductive freedom, sexual liberation as empowerment," said Ms. Greenberg, the pollster. "That is a baby-boom generation way of thinking. If you look at people under 30, that is not their touchstone, it is not wrapped up around feminism and women's rights."

Abortion opponents are reveling in the shift and hope to capitalize. "Not only is this the post-Roe generation, I'd also call it the post-sonogram generation," said Charmaine Yoest, president of Americans United for Life, who notes that baby's first video now occurs in the womb, often accompanied by music. "They can take the video and do the music and send it to the grandmother. We don't even talk anymore about the hypothesis that having an abortion is like having an appendectomy. All of this informs the political pressures on Capitol Hill."

TAUBA AUERBACH

The pressures relating to abortion had seemed, for a time, to go dormant. Mr. Obama, who campaigned on a vow to transcend "the culture wars," even managed to win confirmation of a new Supreme Court justice, Sonia Sotomayor, without the usual Washington abortion uproar. Most of his political energy around abortion has been spent trying to forge consensus on ways to reduce unintended pregnancies.

The quiet was shattered this month, when the House — with surprising support from 64 Democrats — amended its health care bill to include language by Representative Bart Stupak, Democrat of Michigan, barring the use of federal subsidies for insurance plans that cover abortion. Lawmakers like Ms. Slaughter, who advocate for abortion rights, found themselves in the uncomfortable position of voting for the larger health bill even though the Stupak language was in it.

Proponents of the Stupak language say they are simply following existing federal law, which already bars taxpayer financing for abortions. Democratic leaders want a less restrictive provision that would require insurance companies to segregate federal money from private premiums, which could be used to purchase plans that cover abortion.

Representative Debbie Wasserman Schultz, Democrat of Florida and chief deputy whip of the House, blames what she calls the complacency of her own generation for the political climate that allowed Mr. Stupak to prevail. At 43, the mother of three children, she has taken up the abortion rights cause in Congress, as she did as a state legislator.

But if she had to round up her own friends "to go down to the courthouse steps and rally for choice," she said, she is not certain she could. When older women have warned that reproductive rights are being eroded, she said, "basically my generation and younger have looked at them as crying wolf."

That is not to say all younger women are indifferent. Serena Freewomyn (a name she adopted to reflect the idea that "I don't belong to any man") is a 27-year-old administrative assistant at an H.I.V. service provider in Tucson who was inspired, she said, by reading "The War on Choice" by Gloria Feldt. When George Tiller, a doctor in Kansas who performed abortions, was killed in May, she started a blog, Feminists for Choice.

"I think that a lot of younger women do take for granted the fact that they've come of age in a time of post-Roe v. Wade, where they have access to lots of different birth control options," Ms. Freewomyn said. "But I don't think it's fair to say younger women are not engaged; I think younger women are mobilizing in different ways than what people in current leadership positions are used to."

On Wednesday, a coalition calling itself "Stop Stupak" will hold a "National Day of Action" to lobby lawmakers. It will include abortion rights advocacy groups that have sprung up in recent years to reach out to younger voters. Law Students for Reproductive Justice, founded in 2003, will host an Internet seminar to educate law students on the fine points of the House and Senate bills. There's also Choice USA, which targets people under 30. Kierra Johnson, the group's executive director, is pairing up with counterparts in the immigrant rights and gay rights movements — tactics she says are necessary if young people are to be drawn in to the reproductive rights cause. "The same young people who are fighting to keep anti-abortion language out of the health care bills are also fighting to insure that lesbian, gay, bisexual, transgender people fit in to broader health care reform, making sure that immigrant women don't fall through the cracks," she said. "They're coming at these issues in a much more complex way."

The question now is whether the Stop Stupak coalition can succeed. Ms. Wasserman Schultz sees the debate as a chance to rouse women of all generations, and Ms. Slaughter warns that if Mr. Obama signs a bill including the amendment, it will be challenged in court. She says she has worried for years about what would happen "when my generation was gone."

At the moment, her concern has diminished. "Right now, I've never seen women so angry," Ms. Slaughter said. "And the people that were angriest with me were my three daughters."

Legal Fight Could Make Kentucky Only State With No Abortion Clinic

BY SHERYL GAY STOLBERG | MAY 2, 2017

LOUISVILLE, KY. — As states across the nation enact increasingly aggressive restrictions on abortion, perhaps nowhere has the political climate shifted as much as here in Kentucky, where the E.M.W. Women's Surgical Center, a squat tan brick building on Market Street, is the state's sole abortion clinic.

Over the past year, Gov. Matt Bevin, a Republican who calls himself "unapologetically pro-life," has blocked a new Planned Parenthood clinic from performing abortions, shuttered E.M.W.'s satellite clinic in Lexington and threatened to close the existing one in Louisville. Backed by the American Civil Liberties Union, the clinic has sued the state; a trial is set for September.

The governor's forceful moves have rattled reproductive rights advocates, made him a hero among abortion opponents and prompted both sides in the debate to ask a question: Could Kentucky become America's only state to lack a single abortion clinic?

"Kentucky literally stands on the verge of making redemptive history," said the Rev. Rusty Thomas, director of Operation Save America, a Dallas-based anti-abortion group that will host its annual national meeting in Louisville in July. "It could be the first surgically abortion-free state in the United States of America."

Dr. Ernest Marshall, 66, who founded E.M.W. in 1981 and has performed abortions here for 37 years, portrayed the situation from his perspective this way: "We are under assault."

Across the country, the number of abortion providers has been steadily dropping for decades, partly because of better access to birth control — which means fewer unplanned pregnancies, and thus fewer abortions — but also because of restrictions that make it difficult for clinics to stay open.

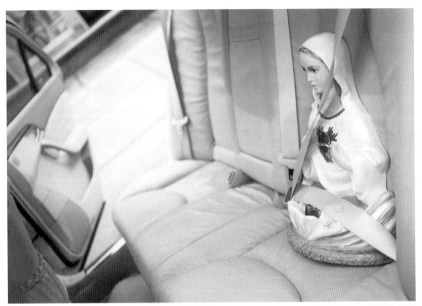

A statue of the Virgin Mary in the back seat of an anti-abortion demonstrator's car outside the E.M.W. Women's Surgical Center in Louisville.

Kentucky, which had 17 abortion providers in 1978, is today among seven states — the others are North Dakota, South Dakota, Missouri, Mississippi, Wyoming and West Virginia — with just one.

Mr. Bevin's election in 2015 was only the beginning of the shift in the abortion landscape here. Republicans, riding Donald J. Trump's coattails, took control of the Kentucky House in November for the first time in 95 years. Their first order of business in January was to pass two measures restricting abortion — one banning the procedure after 20 weeks into a pregnancy, and the other requiring doctors to narrate ultrasounds in detail, regardless of patients' wishes.

The A.C.L.U. is also challenging the ultrasound measure, on the grounds that it violates doctors' First Amendment rights. In signing it, Mr. Bevin vowed to "end this scourge that is the taking of innocent life," adding, "Kentucky will lead the way."

For Elizabeth Nash, who tracks state abortion legislation for the

Guttmacher Institute, a nonprofit research organization, Kentucky's turnabout is striking. "Kentucky for a long time was not on the policy radar," Ms. Nash said. "Now Kentucky is following the model of Texas and Ohio, where they are adopting restrictions or making it very difficult to keep clinic doors open."

At 7:30 in the morning, every Tuesday through Saturday, Kentucky's intensifying battle over abortion plays out in downtown Louisville, along the sidewalk in front of the E.M.W. clinic.

The clinic's mirrored doors are guarded by a volunteer corps of orange-vested escorts, who station themselves strategically at street corners so they can usher patients to the center from nearby parking lots, past a phalanx of protesters.

Men in ball caps finger rosary beads and recite the Lord's Prayer. Some hold grisly signs depicting bloody fetuses or shout religious messages through megaphones. On a recent weekday morning, a young woman arrived, accompanied by her grandmother and carrying a toddler in her arms.

"You're bringing a baby into an abortion clinic!" a man shouted, as escorts hustled them inside. "Where they're going to murder the other baby!"

Inside the clinic, soothing music played. Eleven patients were scheduled that day, roughly half for "medical abortions" in which pills are used to induce miscarriage. One by one, they visited with the clinic's director and counselor, Anne Ahola, who joined the center 17 years ago after working with abused children.

Kentucky law requires that women receive counseling, either in person or by video, at least 24 hours before an abortion. Their stories offered a glimpse into the varied reasons, and often painful decisions, involved in ending pregnancies — especially in a state like Kentucky, where, Dr. Marshall said, many of his colleagues in obstetrics and gynecology oppose abortion.

One 37-year-old woman tearfully confessed that she had had an affair with a co-worker, who was married: "I'm his boss, and this is strictly forbidden; we could both lose our jobs." She quietly asked for a copy of her ultrasound picture.

Another, 29, appeared nonchalant. "I'm working," she said flatly. "It's not in my plan right now."

A third, 31 and a mother of two, said she was trying to escape an abusive relationship. "It's been a struggle for me," she told Ms. Ahola. "I am a religious person, I've been crying and battling with my beliefs, but I also think God understands." She said she worried that the clinic would close: "We need this option."

Ms. Ahola ended each talk with the same question: "Are you sure this is the right decision for you, and did you reach this decision yourself?"

Reproductive rights advocates say women in Kentucky, especially those in poor rural parts of the state, have long faced economic and geographic barriers to obtaining abortions. Many cannot afford to travel or to pay for the procedure. And as surrounding states have enacted restrictions, their options are narrowing.

"We used to have people who lived in Bowling Green; the Nashville clinic was closer than Louisville," said Patricia Canon, who volunteers with the Kentucky Health Justice Network, a nonprofit that helps women pay for abortions and transports them to clinics. "But then Tennessee decided to enact a 48-hour, in-person waiting period. That means two trips, two days."

Yet until recently, advocates hoped abortion services would expand in Kentucky.

When Mr. Bevin's Democratic predecessor, Gov. Steve Beshear, was in office, Planned Parenthood built a new health care center in Louisville. After Mr. Bevin became governor, the center briefly offered abortions, following standard state procedures to obtain a license, said Tamarra Wieder, a spokeswoman for Planned Parenthood here.

The Bevin administration promptly sued, claiming the center was performing abortions illegally. A judge dismissed the case, but the state appealed. So while the Planned Parenthood center is open and

A demonstrator, Joseph Spurgeon, used a microphone to speak to women outside the waiting room of the E.M.W. Women's Surgical Center.

offers an array of reproductive health services, it is obeying the state's "cease and desist" order not to perform abortions.

"For a state as big as Kentucky, one abortion provider is not enough," Ms. Wieder said.

Dr. Marshall's conflict with the state began about a year ago, when state inspectors showed up at his Lexington clinic, which he says operated as a physician's office and thus did not require a license. The state insisted it did.

A legal battle ensued, but as the case dragged on, E.M.W. in Lexington could not afford to stay open without seeing patients, and its landlord refused to renew its lease, said Dona Wells, the former clinic administrator. It closed in January.

The Kentucky National Organization for Women declared the clinic "a permanent casualty" of the governor, while abortion opponents, long beleaguered under Governor Beshear, cheered.

"Kentucky is a very pro-life state," said Mike Janocik, assistant director of the Kentucky to Right Life Association. "Abortion providers tend to fly under the radar, especially when they are in administrations favorable to their position, as ours has been for a long time in Kentucky."

The dispute in Louisville revolves around the state's assertion that E.M.W. lacks adequate "transfer agreements" with hospitals and ambulance services to get women help in case of medical emergency. Amanda Stamper, a spokeswoman for Mr. Bevin, said the governor was "working diligently to protect the health, welfare and lives of women in Kentucky."

But Donald Cox, a lawyer for the Louisville clinic, said the state's complaint was rooted in a technicality: A Catholic health care organization, part owner of the nearby University of Louisville Hospital, will not sign the center's longstanding agreements because of religious objections to abortion.

Last month, the state threatened to close E.M.W. within 10 days; Judge Greg N. Stivers of United States District Court here issued an emergency order blocking the closing, writing that the clinic had "a strong likelihood of success."

The case will be an early test of how federal courts interpret a 2016 Supreme Court ruling, in which the justices struck down parts of a Texas law that imposed similar requirements to Kentucky's, saying they posed an "undue burden" on women, said Brigitte Amiri, a lawyer with the A.C.L.U.'s Reproductive Freedom Project, which also represents the clinic.

"The burden on women in Kentucky if E.M.W. closed down would be extreme," Ms. Amiri said. "There would be an effective ban on abortion."

CHAPTER 3

Pro-Life vs. Pro-Choice

After Roe v. Wade, advocates for abortion rights and those who were staunchly opposed to them continued to protest for or against access to abortion. Those who advocated for a woman's right to choose abortion became known as "pro-choice," while those opposed became known as "pro-life." Advocate groups such as Naral began to take a more political approach, while free speech and religious views were often at play in pro-life protests, with radical groups such as Operation Rescue protesting abortion to the point of violent activity at abortion clinics. As the 21st century approached, advances in science and technology played a larger role in each side's agenda.

Abortion Rights Backers Adopt Tactics of Politics

BY E. J. DIONNE JR. | **JULY 21, 1989**

WASHINGTON, JULY 20 — At the urging of a small army of poll takers, media advisers and consultants, leaders of the abortion rights movement have modified their message to appeal to the millions of Americans who feel deep conflict about abortion and are uneasy with some of the movement's old arguments.

The effort is fueled by hundreds of thousands of dollars poured into polling and advertising. Kate Michelman, president of the National

Abortion Rights Action League, or Naral, says the effort is modeled after a modern political campaign.

The new approach of the abortion rights movement illustrates an important trend in politics: causes, no less than candidates, now must worry about the arcane arts of "framing a message" and "positioning."

Both sides in the abortion battle are aware of this. But abortion rights advocates, particularly Naral, have gone further than their foes in using the new political technologies.

ABORTION FOES ARE CONFIDENT

David O'Steen, executive director of the National Right to Life Committee, says his organization sees itself far ahead in grass-roots organizing. He says that while his side has conducted some polling, it sees little need to change its overall approach.

On the abortion rights side, one of the main results of the strategic reappraisal has been an increased emphasis on a message that draws on the anti-government mood of the Reagan era. The new theme is that the battle over the legality of abortion is less about abortion itself than over whether the government will decide who can have one.

Naral's roster of consultants reads like that of the most sophisticated political campaign. Harrison Hickman, the Democratic poll taker, said he had been paid more than $100,000 for a series of polls. Another Democratic poll taker, Celinda Lake, has also done research.

IMMEDIATE ACTION TAKEN

Frank Greer, a Democratic media consultant, has made television and radio spots for an advertising campaign that has already cost $1.75 million to $2 million. Tony Podesta, who ran Gov. Michael S. Dukakis's Presidential campaign in California, is on retainer as a consultant, at $6,250 a month.

Gina Glantz, field director in Walter F. Mondale's 1984 Presidential campaign, is organizing at the grass roots. And Page Gardner, formerly of the Democratic Senatorial Campaign Committee, is overseeing the operation, acting in effect as a campaign manager.

The mark of the political professionals can be seen not only when money is spent, but also when it is raised. Within hours of the Supreme Court's July 3 ruling in a Missouri case giving the states powers to restrict abortion, the computers at the direct mail firm of Craver, Matthews & Smith in Falls Church, Va., were at work.

They were beaming messages to mailing houses around the country for 900,000 letters seeking money for four organizations that support abortion rights. These were Naral, Planned Parenthood, the National Organization for Women and the American Civil Liberties Union. By Friday, said Roger Craver, president of the firm, 10 million pieces had been mailed.

Mr. O'Steen of the National Right to Life Committee said he was not concerned about the campaigns for abortion rights. "I've been though many waves of advertising during which it was said a pro-abortion giant would stand up," Mr. O'Steen said. "I've never seen it stand up."

And he scoffed at the approach of his opponents. "Their strategy has always been to focus on anything but abortion, to focus attention away from the unborn child," he said.

Burke Balch, the state legislative coordinator for the Right to Life Committee, said that with many polls showing a majority of Americans willing to support some restrictions, his side had a chance to win broad support for regulations that fall short of an outright ban. At the same time, Mr. Balch said, his side can cast the abortion rights movement's opposition to any restrictions as an "extreme" position.

It is precisely to prevent this that the abortion rights cause has hired so many counselors.

LOSING WITH THE PUBLIC

Mr. Greer said the abortion rights advocates, particularly Naral, realized early that no matter how the Supreme Court decided the abortion issue, "they had been losing in the court of public opinion."

Mr. Podesta said, "If abortion is thought of as a selfish or irresponsible act, and if our rhetoric looks frivolous or selfish, you lose a lot of the people in the middle."

Mr. Hickman said both his polling and Ms. Lake's interview sessions with small groups found that while many people were uneasy about abortion, they were even more uneasy about the Government's imposing choices about abortion on individuals.

Mr. Greer said that in group discussions in both North Carolina and Iowa, participants who watched his commercials came to equate restrictions on abortion with Government regulation of gun owners. This, Mr. Greer said, made it clear to him that the abortion rights movement could benefit from the same anti-government mood that has helped so many conservative causes.

STATE OF LIBERTY

Mr. Greer's Naral commercial, televised immediately after the Supreme Court ruling in the Missouri case, featured the Statue of Liberty and a warning that a ban on abortion would violate individual rights and would surrender power to "politicians."

Planned Parenthood has long used the services of one of the nation's best known poll takers, Louis Harris, and the San Francisco-based Public Media Center for advertising.

Faye Wattleton, president of Planned Parenthood, said a poll for her organization a decade ago had convinced her that one of the most popular slogans of the abortion rights movement might be seen by many Americans as too simplistic.

" 'Keep your hands off my body' is a losing argument with the American people," she said. "You have to individualize this debate, you have to make people think about the range of situations people confront and that families confront, and that, most of all, the Government doesn't have an answer to this situation."

TWO GROUPS AS TARGETS

Mr. Greer said the consultants' work on framing a broadly appealing message for the abortion rights side had two targets: those who are wavering, and politicians who might support legal abortion if they see an argument that resonates with the electorate.

Although anti-abortion strategists have not hired high-powered consultants, they are also reviewing the presentation of their message.

"When people focus on abortion itself or the unborn child, they tend to become at least ambivalent and often come to us," Mr. Balch said. "On the other hand, when you focus on the woman, it's an obvious and natural thing to say that, 'I know so-and-so who's had an abortion, and she's a good person, and I don't want to condemn her.' We have to keep focusing on the unborn child."

His comments address what may be the central aspect of the struggle: with so many Americans ambivalent about abortion, the most important battle will be over how the issue is framed.

Drive Against Abortion Finds a Symbol: Wichita

BY ISABEL WILKERSON | AUG. 4, 1991

WICHITA, KAN., AUG. 1 — Much like the tornadoes that Kansans curse but live with, a political windstorm has touched down on this prairie city and hurled it into the center of the bitter national feud over a woman's right to an abortion.

For nearly three weeks now, this city has become the most vivid symbol of an emboldened anti-abortion movement as members of Operation Rescue focus on the city's three abortion clinics, flinging themselves under cars, sitting by the hundreds at clinic doorways and blocking women from entering as they read them Scripture.

The confrontations have resulted in more than 1,600 arrests and the closing of all three abortion clinics for more than a week in late July.

The city has had to assign nearly a quarter of its police force to control the protests, and a Federal judge earlier this week ordered Federal marshals to keep the clinics open.

NO SIGNS OF ABATING

The confrontations show no sign of abating, and some doctors have had to perform abortions in the predawn hours to avoid disruption. Leaders of the protest say they plan to stay indefinitely.

"We have a highly polarized circumstance right now," said Mayor Bob Knight, an avowed opponent of abortion. "This absolutely breaks my heart."

Operation Rescue, the renegade of the anti-abortion lobby, came to Wichita looking for an America of wheatfields and churchgoers, far from the noisy, liberal cities they find hostile. They were looking for a sympathetic ear and a congregation to preach to.

And with their walkie-talkies and hushed game plans, they were also anticipating a fight.

On at least one front, they found what they were looking for. Wichita has one of the few clinics in the country where women can get an abortion in the final three months of pregnancy.

The one-story clinic, Women's Health Care Services, run by Dr. George R. Tiller, has become the lightning rod for the battle.

It is here that women from all over the country come for abortions that few other physicians will perform. Inside the wood-paneled clinic hangs a map of North America, covered, like ants on a sidewalk, with yellow, red, blue and white pins, representing the visits of women from all 50 states and most of the Canadian provinces.

Clinic officials say that of the 2,000 abortions performed here each year, a small number, about 10 or 12, are for women in the third trimester, and they are usually prompted by severe fetal abnormalities or life-threatening risks to themselves. About 35 percent are performed on women in their second trimester, the remainder in the first.

'CITY IS UNDER SIEGE'

What goes on inside the clinic has set off gut-level emotions. Demonstrators stand on both sides of bustling Kellogg Street, holding signs that say, "Babies Killed Here" and "Tiller's Slaughter House," waving to the drivers of Mack trucks and minivans that honk their horns in support as they pass.

At times it has taken 40 police officers, some on horseback, to keep the clinic's doors open. And even then, John Cowles, Dr. Tiller's lawyer said, "protesters shoved their way through and crawled beneath them."

Clinic staff members have had to work 36 straight hours out of fear that if they left, they would not be able to get back in.

"We feel this entire city is under siege," said Peggy Jarman, the clinic's spokeswoman. "Where is the line ever going to be drawn in the name of freedom of speech?"

On July 23, Judge Patrick Kelly of Federal District Court here issued an order prohibiting the protesters from blocking entry to the clinic.

But the next day, the protesters, some praying and singing and reading passages from the Bible, stood at the gate exhorting women not to go in. This week, two protesters even crawled under Dr. Tiller's van to prevent him from driving into the clinic's driveway.

"It is clear that these people will stop at nothing to impose their views on others," said Kate Michelman, president of the National Abortion Rights Action League, a Washington-based advocacy group.

"These are scary people," she said. "This is bleary-eyed zealotry. It's hard to believe we're living in the United States of America. These women are being subjected to tyranny and terrorism."

A WARM RECEPTION

But the protesters see the nation's midsection and Wichita as the defining frontier for the debate over abortion.

"The abortion battle is not going to be decided in the trendy urban centers," said the Rev. Patrick Mahoney, a Presbyterian minister from Boca Raton, Fla., and a spokesman for Operation Rescue.

"It will be decided street by street, town by town, village by village," he said. "Wichita is the heartland of America. In capsule form, Wichita embodies what we will see in the next three to four years."

The protesters say the confrontation here is the beginning of the fight that is building as the Supreme Court moves closer, they say, to overturning Roe v. Wade, the decision that legalized abortion in 1973.

Randall Terry, the onetime used-car salesman who founded the group four years ago and spent a week in jail for violating Judge Kelly's restraining order, said the protest showed "that the rescue movement is alive and well and in full strength."

"The challenge before us is to use this street-level momentum and take back the state legislatures all over the country," he said. "The sky is the limit of the potential here."

Indeed, when Mr. Terry's followers gather at clinics in places like Los Angeles, more people show up to protest them than to protest abortion. But here, Operation Rescue has had the stage virtually to itself.

"We've never seen anything like it," Mr. Terry said. "People have just sprung to action for our cause. We had no idea we would be received so warmly."

John Snow, a retired accountant, was one of the people who showed up, not to get arrested particularly, but just to show his support. He sat on the sidewalk across from the clinic, dispensing Kool-Aid and saying the rosary.

"They're in there killing babies, nothing else, ma'am," Mr. Snow said. "You hear those cars honking. You know what that means? The people are with us."

The protesters go about their work with the determination of soldiers, with round-the-clock reconnaissance, taking delight in knowledge of the enemy's moves. "We know when Tiller's using the bathroom," said Jeff White, the group's tactical director. "Tiller has moved people in at 3 in the morning. He's not free to do it in the light of day."

Dr. Tiller, a 49-year-old family physician and former Navy flight surgeon, has been performing abortions for 17 years. He declined to comment, his lawyer said, to avoid enflaming the situation.

Abortion rights advocates say they fear that what the anti-abortion groups are doing in Wichita may be repeated all over the tradition-bound expanse between the coasts.

"All of these groups have found a legitimacy they didn't have before," Ms. Michelman said.

Prof. John Stanga, chairman of the political science department at Wichita State University, said that however the protest ends, people in Wichita, which has already spent about $400,000 to keep the clinics open, have had enough of it.

"The community is ready for them to go home, to Fargo, N.D., or wherever they're going next," he said.

Face of Protests in Wichita Is Religious and Undoubting

BY DON TERRY | **AUG. 12, 1991**

WICHITA, KAN., AUG. 11 — For three days, David Spear drove the 1,700 miles here from his home in San Francisco as fast as his old car would go.

He made the trip with little food, sleep or money, he said, because "the Holy Spirit led me here" to join what has become a monthlong assault on the city's three abortion clinics.

It has been a month of protests, prayers and police, a month that has brought national attention to Wichita along with hundreds of abortion opponents like Mr. Spear, a 42-year-old street artist, shoe shiner and window washer.

"I don't dislike pro-choice people," he said. "Some of my best friends are pro-choice and I pray for them. All I want is the law changed. I want babies to live. It won't be easy though because Satan is all around us."

The protests, organized by the militant anti-abortion group Operation Rescue, have resulted in nearly 2,000 arrests since late July. A Federal judge, who issued an order forbidding them to block access to two of the clinics, has received numerous threats and is under round-the-clock protection.

Slightly more than half of those arrested have been from Kansas.

Mr. Spear and the others have come from big cities and small towns, from unemployment lines and steady jobs, from Lansing, Mich., from Boston, from Dayton, Ohio, from Miami, from Portland, Ore. They see themselves, in the words of Mr. Spear, as "warriors of prayer" in a civil war over abortion.

To them the issue is clear and very simple. Abortion, they say, is murder and if it continues much longer America will suffer God's judgment.

"I'm surprised God hasn't allowed another nation to take us over yet," said Gladys Mitchell from Michigan.

Many of the abortion opponents who have flocked here since the middle of July, like Pam Schuffert, 39, of Asheville, N.C., or Joe Stauder, 52, of Ann Arbor, Mich., travel from city to city, state to state, to block the gates of abortion clinics with their bodies.

"I've been arrested in Atlanta, Dobbs Ferry, Washington, Charlotte, Greensboro, Asheville and a couple of other places," Miss Schuffert said. "I still have 10 days to serve in Greensboro and 36 hours in Charlotte."

Before coming to Wichita, Miss Schuffert said, she had just been in jail in Raleigh, N.C., after a protest there.

"I'm weary," she said the other day as she prepared to rush the gate of a clinic here. The campaign in Wichita, she said, "is my 16th rescue," using the term that members of the anti-abortion movement favor for their efforts.

The authorities call it law breaking, and according to results of a survey released today by The Wichita Eagle and KAKE-TV, 78 percent of the 483 Sedgwick County residents surveyed disapproved of the protesters' tactics, and 52 percent said they believed that the city's image had been damaged by the weeks of unrest. The survey, taken Wednesday and Thursday in random telephone calls, has a margin of sampling error of 4.5 percentage points.

On Monday some of the protesters, including a founder of Operation Rescue, the Rev. Joseph Foreman, are scheduled to appear before Judge Patrick F. Kelly of Federal District Court on charges of violating his order.

"A judge's order won't stop us," Mr. Foreman said before being arrested Friday and held on $100,000 bond.

FRIENDLY RECEPTION

Despite the poll's findings, the protesters have received a friendlier reception in Wichita, a city of 300,000, than they have in larger cities.

Operation Rescue and its out-of-town followers have set up camp at the Wichita Plaza Hotel downtown, where a spokesman for the group, Gary McCullogh, said they had at least 40 rooms.

He said the hotel had halved its rate for the group to $25 a room, most of which are shared by four adults.

Other protesters have moved in for a few nights with families here, and several churches have turned their basements into dormitories.

There have been other signs of hospitality rarely offered to the group in larger cities. At a recent rally, the state's Governor, Joan Finney, a Democrat, spoke warmly of its effort.

"I am pro-life," she proclaimed to the cheers of 1,500 people.

For the most part, getting here was not easy for many of the protesters, mainly blue-collar workers like sign painters, store clerks and truck drivers. Mr. Stauder, of Ann Arbor, was a school janitor until he quit his job almost three years ago to devote full time to abortion protests.

The protesters travel in groups and pay for gasoline and food by saving pennies or by soliciting donations from church groups or relatives back home.

"I live very simply," Mr. Stauder said. "I have a brother who gives me $200 a month. I live and travel on that."

But among their ranks are also school teachers on vacation, medical technicians on their lunch breaks, retired couples and newlyweds.

"The rescuers seem like average folk," said Steve Grantstien, a 38-year-old nuclear medicine technician from Wichita and, he said, one of the few Jews taking part in the protests. "It seems like 30 percent of them are retired."

DR. KING AND JOHN BROWN

The leaders are mostly male and from out of town. They sprinkle their conversation with references to the Rev. Dr. Martin Luther King Jr., the civil rights movement, the Holocaust and, because this is Kansas, John Brown.

Nuns, priests and ministers kneel at the rallies, fingering rosaries or clutching Bibles before leading a charge against the clinics' gates. Some have been dragged off to jail as many as six times.

The women, young and old, are "Mrs." or "Miss," rarely "Ms."

"We don't accept that term," said 33-year-old Stephanie Hunley, a Mrs. from Dayton. "It's a feminist term."

NEARLY ALL WHITE

A vast majority of the protesters are white, a fact that apparently causes some concern. After telling a story about persuading a young woman in Dayton not to have an abortion, Mrs. Hunley said, "I'd also like to emphasize that the woman was a black lady."

"I know you don't see a lot of black people out here now," she said without being asked about the lack of black faces in the crowd of several hundred. "But we extend our hand to everyone. We love them, too."

Protesters are stationed almost around the clock outside the Women's Health Care Services, one of the few clinics in the country that performs abortions in the final three months of pregnancy.

Tiffany White, a 19-year-old resident of Wichita, said she became involved with the anti-abortion protests a couple of weeks ago when the guilt and anguish over her own abortion when she was 16 grew overwhelming.

"I was raped," she said. "I didn't even know who the father was. But I loved that baby. I wanted it."

Being young, scared and uncertain, "I turned to my mom." Her mother, she said, forced her to have an abortion, and, "I very much regret it now."

Earlier that day, the street was flooded with 350 abortion opponents, dozens of Federal marshals, local police and a growing band of supporters of the clinics. Even in that crowd, King David Davis, a 34-year-old unemployed father of three from Wichita, stood out in his black karate uniform, monster mask and gloves covered in fake blood. He has worn the costume almost every day for weeks.

"I represent the evil that is going on in there," he said, pointing to the one-story clinic. "Remember, David was a little man with a small rock, and he was able to destroy a mighty giant. Truth will be our rock."

A boy approached him and tugged on his karate uniform. "The police are looking at you," the boy said. "You need to take the mask off."

Abortion Clinics Preparing for More Violence

BY FELICITY BARRINGER | MARCH 12, 1993

WASHINGTON, MARCH 11 — The low-rise suburban landscape that is the setting of most abortion clinics is an unlikely backdrop for martial metaphors and discussions of how to block bullets. But in one small city after another, abortion providers said today that they saw the fatal shooting of their colleague, Dr. David Gunn, on Wednesday as the inevitable result of a moral battle that long ago turned physical.

If abortion opponents see the shooting as an "isolated incident" and the work of a "nutcake," abortion rights advocates — both feminists and the obstetricians who perform 1.6 million abortions each year in the United States — see it as the culmination of a decade or more of blockades, fire bombings, chemical attacks and nighttime gunfire.

Given that history, the slaying of Dr. Gunn in Pensacola, Fla., has become a call to arms among abortion providers who say it is past time to defend themselves and each other.

In Boulder, Colo., it is bullet-proof windows. In Santa Rosa, Calif., abortion rights volunteers are organizing 24-hour watches at clinics. In Fort Wayne, Ind., and Wichita, Kan., abortion clinics employ security guards, as does the Planned Parenthood clinic in Des Moines. The clinic in Kansas City, Mo., hired armed guards today.

Dr. G. W. Orr, an obstetrician who performs abortions in Omaha is getting a bullet-proof vest. So is Dr. Buck Williams in Sioux Falls, S.D., and he is not stopping at that. "Overnight I changed handguns and went from a .38-caliber to a .45," he said. "That'll just make a bigger hole in somebody.

In Milwaukee, Dr. George Woodward went public at a news conference today about the threats he had received as an abortion provider, figuring that high visibility was safer than a low profile. In a later telephone interview he said: "I'm working hand in glove with

Planned Parenthood and the Milwaukee and Brookfield, Wis., police departments, doing everything I can to take every precaution I can. I haven't become a Salman Rushdie yet, but I may."

On the other hand, some abortion providers said there was little more they could realistically hope to do to protect themselves.

In Colorado, Dr. Warren Hern, medical director of the Boulder Abortion Clinic, said: "I am sitting here behind my desk, looking out a bullet-proof window. I work in four layers of bullet-proof windows. Death threats are so common they are not remarkable. I went to a pro-choice meeting in Denver recently, and as I walked through the picket line, someone said, 'You should die.' "

The news of Dr. Gunn's shooting was a wrenching departure from the script of the nation's longest-running public morality play, one that forced the players to rethink their own rote approaches to their roles. While the focus of abortion rights activists was the need for protection and resistance, many abortion opponents, whose movement had been built on appeals to morality, showed palpable anguish over an act of violence in the name of their cause.

ABORTION FOES REACT

Such anguish was not evident in the earliest reactions from groups like Operation Rescue, Rescue America and Missionaries to the Preborn, which mixed often-pallid condemnations of the murder with calls for support funds for the family of Michael F. Griffin, the man accused of killing Dr. Gunn.

In an interview with CBS News, Randall Terry, director of Operation Rescue, said of Dr. Gunn, "While we grieve for him and for his widow and for his children, we must also grieve for the thousands of children that he has murdered."

Debbie Dykes, a member of the American Family Association in Bradenton, said, "I think the man that was killed — and it was unfortunate — he should be glad he was not killed the same way that he has killed other people, which is limb by limb."

Dr. David Gunn.

By contrast, the United States Catholic Conference and some other longtime abortion opponents reacted with rage tempered with sorrow at an act that some felt threatened the moral foundation of their cause.

"The violence of killing in the name of pro-life makes a mockery of the pro-life cause," the conference said in a statement. "As we abhor the violence of abortion, we abhor violence as a dangerous and deplorable means to stop abortion."

The statement added, "It is not enough to say, 'We sympathize with Mr. Griffin's motivations but disagree with his actions.' In the name and in the true spirit of pro-life, we call on all in the pro-life movement to condemn such violence in no uncertain terms."

A SHARED TERM: 'TERRORIST'

Bill Price, president of Texans United for Life, sounded a similar theme. "I'm a little bit disturbed by comments and quotes from colleagues in the pro-life movement which appear to be rationalizing or justifying or minimizing this horrific act," he said.

"I think, frankly, there has been a philosophical or even moral groundwork laid for assassinating abortionists by certain people in the pro-life movement, and I think they bear some of the blame. If they don't stop it, there will be an increase in these kinds of acts. You don't win a moral war through force or coercion or intimidation. You win through reason.

"I think it is a defining point in the history of this struggle," he added. "Responsible leaders have to speak out against this. If they don't, we will just become a bunch of terrorists."

While Douglas Johnson, a spokesman for the National Right to Life Committee, dismissed Mr. Griffin as "a nutcake," abortion rights advocates used Mr. Price's word, "terrorists," in their calls for help from local and state officials and from President Clinton, Congress and the Federal Bureau of Investigation.

CLINTON CONDEMNS SHOOTING

In a statement today, President Clinton said: "I was saddened and angered by the fatal shooting in Pensacola yesterday of Dr. David Gunn. The violence against clinics must stop."

Abortion rights advocates argued that the shooting should give renewed impetus to efforts to pass legislation like the Freedom of Choice Act, which would codify into law the provisions of the Supreme Court's 1973 Roe v. Wade decision legalizing most abortions. They also pushed for passage of a bill now in the House that would make it a Federal crime to interfere with abortion clinics' services to their patients.

Several states are considering similar laws to protect access, and legislators in Tallahassee, Fla., said today that they would speed up consideration of a measure in that state.

Some abortion rights activists argue that the need for such laws increased recently when the Supreme Court ruled that abortion protesters could not be enjoined from blocking access to clinics under a

19th Century law known as the Ku Klux Klan Act, which prohibits conspiracies to deny citizens their constitutional rights. Injunctions under state laws, like those governing trespass, remain in force, though it is not known how many such laws there are.

'HUDDLING TOGETHER FOR WARMTH'

Telephones at clinics rang constantly today, with calls from reporters, from groups like Planned Parenthood and the National Abortion Federation, and from other clinics expressing sympathy and support. "It's mostly huddling together for warmth," said Peg Johnston, an administrator at Southern Tier Women's Services near Binghamton, N.Y., the hometown of Mr. Terry.

Although her clinic has put up a perimeter fence to keep protesters off the property, she said: "I don't think there's any real way to protect yourself against this kind of terrorism. We've all been saying and worrying that the violence was going to escalate."

During a break in a hearing at State District Court in Dallas, where Roe v. Wade was first heard, Dr. Norman Tompkins said he is "very much" concerned about his safety and that of his family after the Florida killing. "It scares the living daylights out of me," he said.

Pro Bono TV Spot for Abortion Rights

BY STUART ELLIOTT | MARCH 1, 1994

AN ABORTION RIGHTS organization and its agency are introducing a pro bono television commercial that is meant to counter a paid anti-abortion campaign introduced almost two years ago.

The abortion rights spot was produced by Mad Dogs and Englishmen, a small New York shop, for the New York State chapter of the National Abortion Rights Action League, or Naral, which will distribute it to the organization's other chapters around the country. It is intended as an answer to much-publicized anti-abortion commercials sponsored by the Arthur S. De Moss Foundation, which carry the theme "Life. What a beautiful choice."

The theme of the Naral commercial: "Choice. What a beautiful life."

"It's important that there is a response to the De Moss ads," said Kelli Conlin, executive director of Naral's New York State chapter. "Both sides need to be represented."

The abortion rights organization's 30-second spot was produced in a no-fuss, low-key fashion, featuring simple, childlike drawings and zippy background music. It contrasts sharply with the warmly emotional, slickly produced De Moss spots. The spot centers on personal preferences in areas like food, religion and hair styles, then segues into the issue of "Whether you have a baby — or an abortion."

Nick Cohen, chairman and creative director at Mad Dogs, said: "We didn't want to do a slanted bit of advertising that says, 'Choose abortion.' We wanted to do a piece that says protect your freedom of choice."

Mr. Cohen said he was inspired to create the spot after watching the De Moss commercials on WCBS, Channel 2 in New York. Martin Blair, a WCBS spokesman, said the Naral spot is "expected to receive a positive response" in terms of being run on an unpaid basis; the spot has also been submitted by Naral to networks like CNN and MTV.

Planned Parenthood Will Offer Early Abortion Procedures

BY **KAREN DEMASTERS** | DEC. 28, 1997

DOCTORS AT THE Planned Parenthood clinics in Trenton and Shrews-bury, the two Planned Parenthood sites in New Jersey where abortions are performed, may be offering a new early-pregnancy abortion procedure by spring.

The procedure, which enables an abortion to be performed as early as seven days after conception, was pioneered by Dr. Jerry Edwards, the Planned Parenthood medical director in Houston, who recently published his research, said the directors of the two clinics.

Until recently, abortions during the earliest stages of pregnancy created a risk because it was difficult to assure a complete abortion and a second procedure was sometimes needed, said Kathy Gunkel, associate executive director of Planned Parenthood of Central Jersey, which operates the Shrewsbury clinic.

Doctors from the clinics here and elsewhere across the country will be trained in Houston and each will start the new procedure on its own time schedule, said Leslie Davis Potter, Planned Parenthood executive director for the Mercer County area.

The Partial-Birth Stratagem

EDITORIAL | BY THE NEW YORK TIMES | MAY 16, 1998

DOCTORS IN WISCONSIN stopped performing abortions on Thursday when Judge John Shabaz of the Federal District Court refused to issue a temporary restraining order against the state's newly enacted "partial birth" abortion ban. The doctors quickly concluded that performing any type of abortion in Wisconsin would subject them to prosecution and possible life imprisonment under that law. After all, the point of this kind of partial-birth ban is to end access to abortion in general.

The ban's proponents cloak their strategy by directing attention to a rare medical procedure used in late-term abortions called "intact dilation and extraction." But the actual language of the law says nothing about that particular procedure, nor does it say anything about late-term abortions. The wording, broad enough to cover the most common procedures, prohibits any abortion in which a doctor "partially vaginally delivers a living child, causes the death of the partially delivered child with the intent to kill the child and then completes the delivery of the child." "Child" is defined as "a human being from the time of fertilization" until birth. That description could apply to any first or second trimester abortion in which fetal tissue is expelled from the uterus into the vagina.

Such a ban on abortions prior to fetal viability is unconstitutional under Roe v. Wade. The statute also allows no exception to protect the woman's health, which is required under Roe for bans that would apply to abortions after fetal viability. This law is a direct assault on the right to choose abortion as a private medical decision, and Wisconsin is not alone. Some 28 states have enacted laws with nearly identical language. Only two have even bothered to restrict the ban to post-viability abortions. Judges in many states have blocked these copy-cat statutes because they are clearly unconstitutional. The

Federal partial-birth bill, which has been vetoed twice by President Clinton, is expected to come up for a veto override vote later this year.

Judge Shabaz, in unjustly denying the request to block the law temporarily, nonetheless wrote that the opponents of the ban seem likely to prevail on the merits when the case is heard in June. But in the meantime, women in Wisconsin will be denied timely medical care. The situation is glaring proof of the true nature of the partial-birth strategy.

'Partial Birth' Deceptions

EDITORIAL | BY THE NEW YORK TIMES | OCT. 20, 1999

ONCE AGAIN A woman's right to choose abortion is under direct attack in Congress. The Senate is poised to vote today on the latest Congressional attempt to impose a national ban on so-called partial birth abortions. Billed by its proponents as a narrow targeting of a single late-term procedure, the measure is actually a backdoor attempt to severely constrict abortion rights throughout all stages of pregnancy.

This reality has not been lost on the courts. Since the Senate's last partial birth vote, there have been 11 court decisions on the legal merits of partial birth bans passed by different states. In all but one instance, the ban was blocked because of constitutional problems.

Just last month the United States Court of Appeals for the Eighth Circuit struck down partial birth statutes in Nebraska, Arkansas and Iowa. Two of the statutes included language nearly identical to the language of the Senate bill. Finding that the term "partial birth abortion" has no fixed medical or legal meaning, the court said that the vague laws placed an undue burden on abortion rights by outlawing even the safest and most common procedures used before fetal viability.

Of course, Republican leaders are well aware of what the courts have been saying. But that has not prevented them from forging ahead without holding a single hearing on the serious constitutional issues. The real goal here is to gain an edge in next year's election by forcing President Clinton to lift his veto pen for the third time. The nation's lawmakers should have more respect for the Constitution, women's rights and their own institution than to go along with such a dangerous and deceptive game.

Anti-Abortion Site on Web Has Ignited Free Speech Debate

BY SAM HOWE VERHOVEK | JAN. 13, 1999

PORTLAND, ORE., JAN. 12 — "The Nuremberg Files: Visualize Abortionists on Trial," proclaims the site on the World Wide Web. With simulated blood dripping from fetus parts, the site leads a cyber-visitor to the "main archive," listing the names of dozens of doctors and clinic workers around the country who provide abortions.

For some of the people the site calls "baby butchers," the information includes photographs, home addresses, license plate numbers, the names of their spouses and children. A few doctors, including Barnett A. Slepian of Amherst, N.Y., near Buffalo, who was fatally shot by a sniper last fall, have a line through their names, denoting that they have been killed; those who have been wounded have their names listed in gray.

For a Federal court jury here, hearing a civil case brought by Planned Parenthood and several doctors against some of the most militant abortion opponents in the country, the trial will boil down to this question: is the Web site constitutionally protected free speech?

The plaintiffs, who are seeking up to $200 million in damages, have brought their case under the 1994 Federal Freedom of Access to Clinic Entrances Act, which makes it illegal to use "force or threat of force" against anyone seeking or providing an abortion, and allows clinics to seek unlimited damages if workers are harmed or intimidated. But as simple as the question before the jury sounds, the legal issues are not.

For one thing, this is the first major case brought under the law that does not involve direct personal threats or an actual physical confrontation. While the plaintiffs say the Web site amounts to a solicitation of murder, the defendants contend that it is a legal informational tool.

The Web site, which is named for the German city in which Nazis were put on trial after World War II, explains: "A coalition of concerned citizens throughout the U.S.A. is cooperating in collecting dossiers on abortionists in anticipation that one day we may be able to hold them on trial for crimes against humanity. We anticipate the day when these people will be charged in perfectly legal courts once the tide of this nation's opinion turns against the wanton slaughter of God's children."

But abortion is legal. And in the climate surrounding the issue — the National Abortion Federation says there have been 7 killings, 15 attempted murders, 99 acid attacks, 154 arson incidents and 39 bombings involving abortion clinics or workers in the last two decades — the plaintiffs here say that radical anti-abortion groups are clearly using devices like the Web site to incite more violence and deny women access to abortion services.

"Just like bounty hunters of the Old West, the defendants want to stop the doctors by any means — dead in their tracks," Maria Vullo, a lawyer for the plaintiffs, told jurors. "It's terrorism."

In testimony here on Monday, Dr. Warren Hern, of Boulder, Colo., said his life had been turned into a nightmare by the protesters, who have also put his face on their "Deadly Dozen" flier, which looks like a wanted poster and says he and other doctors are "Guilty of Crimes Against Humanity."

"It has made me feel a great sense of personal isolation," Dr. Hern told the jurors, explaining that he now wears a bulletproof vest, covers his windows, always sits with his back toward the wall and is leery of any contact with strangers.

But the roster of 14 defendants, which includes the American Coalition of Life Advocates, an umbrella group that has been described as too extreme by more mainstream anti-abortion groups, say most of the information they provide could be found in telephone directories.

Furthermore, they say, nothing in the "Nuremberg Files" advocates violence against the doctors or clinic workers, although the site does include links to other Web pages that defend killing abortion workers as legally justifiable homicide, and to a letter from prison from Paul J. Hill, who murdered a doctor in Pensacola, Fla., in 1994. In it, he describes "the joy I felt after shooting the abortionist, and still feel today."

In opening arguments last week, Chris Ferrara, a lawyer for the defendants, said the case was baseless. "This is a case about the threat to kill or injure, which is simply not there," he said. "Opinions? Yes, sometimes harsh. But no violence."

Judge Robert E. Jones of Federal District Court, has turned down requests from the defendants to dismiss the case outright, in effect ruling that the Web site was not automatically protected free speech.

In some ways, Judge Jones seems to have signaled that the plaintiffs may have a valid case. Quoting an appeals court ruling in another case, Judge Jones wrote that "alleged threats should be considered in light of their entire factual context, including the surrounding events and the reaction of the listeners."

Jonathan Entin, a law professor at Case Western Reserve University in Cleveland, said the case posed a difficult question of where to draw the line between protected free speech and illegal threats. The basic standard set by the Supreme Court is that speech is protected unless it is directed toward and likely to produce "imminent lawless action," he said.

"The problem for the plaintiffs is, the Web site does not explicitly say, it is your moral duty to go out and kill these people or maim them or harm their family," Professor Entin said. "On the other hand, in the context in which this case is being litigated, we know there are people who are out there who are willing to go out and kill people who perform abortions. So the question is, to what extent will people take seriously the implicit message on this Web site, which is clearly that all right-thinking people should use whatever means necessary to stop people from performing abortions?"

Other experts said that if the Web site specifically advocated murder, it would almost certainly be found to be illegal, and, conversely, if it did not list doctors' names and addresses, it would almost certainly be considered protected speech. But the question before the jury, where in the middle does it belong?

"The issues in this case are very tricky," said David J. Fidanque, executive director of the American Civil Liberties Union of Oregon, which has filed a friend-of-the-court brief, arguing that the jury must focus not only on the fear the list may have spurred in the doctors, but also on the intent of the abortion opponents who contributed to it.

Though the case happens to represent one of the first major jury trials regarding free speech and threats on the Internet, several legal experts agreed that the core issue would be the same if the abortion opponents had published the list of doctors in a newspaper or flier.

The plaintiffs want an injunction from Judge Jones that could essentially force the abortion opponents to cease circulating the files. Among the named defendants are Michael Bray, a minister and author of a book called "A Time to Kill," which argues that killings of abortion doctors can be justifiable, and C. Roy McMillan, director of an anti-abortion group in Mississippi who has said that "it wouldn't bother me if every abortionist in the country today fell dead from a bullet."

In testimony this afternoon, another defendant, Andrew Burnett, publisher of Life Advocate Magazine of Portland, defended publishing the names and addresses of doctors on the Web site with the address www.christiangallery.com/atrocity. He said his own address had been published numerous times in The Oregonian, the daily newspaper in Portland, after he was arrested in abortion protests.

It was a jarring experience, Mr. Burnett said, but one that made him realize how committed he was to his cause. Of the lists, he said: "It's a legitimate way to have people reconsider what they do for a living."

Religious Searching Leads to the Anti-Abortion Movement

BY JOHN KIFNER | MARCH 30, 2001

THEY CALLED HIM "Atomic Dog."

That was the name that James C. Kopp, arrested yesterday in the 1998 sniper slaying of Barnett A. Slepian, a doctor who provided abortions in Amherst, N.Y., took a dozen years ago during a fateful, formative, 40-day stretch in an Atlanta jail.

At the height of the anti-abortion movement's efforts to blockade clinics, and with national attention focused on the 1988 Democratic Convention, Randall Terry's Operation Rescue had declared a siege of Atlanta. More than a hundred protesters, arrested as they blocked clinic entrances and intersections, were packed into a wing of the Key Road Detention Facility. In defiant noncooperation, they refused to give their real names to the authorities.

The atmosphere inside the jail was intense, fervid, according to people who were held there, with daylong preaching and prayers deepening devotion to their cause. For some, the spiritual experience was so powerful that they became the nucleus of a more violent anti-abortion movement.

Alongside Mr. Kopp were Rachelle Shannon, who would shoot a doctor in Wichita, Kan.; John Arena, convicted of dousing clinics with butyric acid, a respiratory poison; Andrew Cabot, one of the signers of a declaration calling the killing of abortion providers "justifiable homicide"; and the Rev. Norman Weslin, founder of an itinerant band of Roman Catholic protesters known as the Lambs of Christ.

"For Kopp, and for many other people, it was a lot like the Bolsheviks being in the czar's prison," Mark Potok, who traces extremist organizations for the Southern Poverty Law Center, said yesterday. "It really did turn the jail into a school for revolutionaries."

One of the products of the jail was an anonymously written 113-page booklet called the "Manual of the Army of God" — a copy was found buried in Ms. Shannon's backyard — with instructions on how to make C-4 plastic explosives, homemade ammonium nitrate bombs like the one used in Oklahoma City, and the suggestion that doctors providing abortions should have their hands cut off. The first name on a list of acknowledgments is "Atomic Dog."

The introduction declares: "This is a manual for those who have come to understand that the battle against abortion is a battle not against flesh and blood, but against the devil and all the evil he can muster among flesh and blood to fight at his side."

Before he was arrested yesterday in France, investigators said, Mr. Kopp had been living in Ireland, working at clerical jobs and moving from place to place.

It seems a long and strange path for a shy, quiet young man who grew up skateboarding in Marin County, Calif., north of San Francisco, an Eagle scout and a trombone player in his high school band. At the sunny campus of the University of California at Santa Cruz, where he lived off campus with his girlfriend, Jennifer, he earned a degree in marine biology in 1976. He also holds a master's in biology.

But beginning around 1984, along with an increasing obsession with religion, Mr. Kopp's life began to be marked by a series of arrests in anti-abortion protests.

A crucial event, in addition to his parents' bitter divorce, appears to have been the abortion that Jennifer — his relatives have only used her first name — had before she and Mr. Kopp broke up.

"His father confided to me that Jim was very, very upset about it," his stepmother, Lynn Kopp, told The New York Times Magazine in 1999. "He was upset because it was his child and he was not consulted. It just broke him. When he found out about it, it just flipped him out."

Increasingly, he turned to religion. It was a search that would take him to the retreat in the Swiss Alps of Francis Schaeffer, the founder of modern Protestant fundamentalism, and to missions in South America and the Philippines, where he honed his skills as a construction worker.

Abandoning his Lutheran roots, he converted to Catholicism, dreaming of becoming a priest. But, family members said, the order he wanted to join turned him down. Beginning on April 8, 1984, Mr. Kopp was arrested nine times outside San Francisco clinics on charges ranging from trespass to aggravated assault.

In 1986, he moved to the Bronx, joining the Missionaries of Charity, an order founded by Mother Teresa, where he rose every morning at 4:30 to feed the homeless and crack addicts in the order's soup kitchens.

But more and more, he became obsessed with the abortion issue. In 1988 he moved to Binghamton, N.Y., where Mr. Terry, an evangelical street preacher, was running Operation Rescue, which mounted blockades of abortion clinics and other civil disobedience protests. Mr. Terry quickly adopted him as a liaison to the Catholic wing of the protest movement and a key aide.

Mr. Kopp was a pioneer in a strategy of locking protesters together or to buildings to make it more difficult for the police to remove them.

After the Atlanta demonstrations, Mr. Kopp also protested frequently with the Lambs of Christ, the group headed by Father Weslin, a charismatic former paratroop officer turned priest. During demonstrations in Rochester, some protesters locked themselves into a device called "the oven," which was constructed from metal and concrete and had to be carried off in a truck.

In 1994, Congress passed the Freedom of Access to Clinic Entrances Law, which made it a crime to obstruct clinics and provided tough penalties if anyone was hurt during demonstrations. While clinic blockades and mass arrests dropped to almost nil, since 1993 there have been seven murders of doctors and other clinic workers — something previously unheard of — along with 14 attempted murders and many incidents involving bombing, arson and vandalism.

Mr. Kopp himself is a suspect in three nonfatal ambushes of doctors in Canada, and another in a Rochester suburb, the authorities say.

After Stem-Cell Rift, Groups Unite for Anti-Abortion Push

BY KEVIN SACK WITH GUSTAV NIEBUHR | SEPT. 4, 2001

ATLANTA, SEPT. 3 — Seeking to show a united front after deep divisions over embryonic stem cell research, a coalition of socially conservative groups plans to kick off a campaign this week to pressure President Bush and the Democratic-controlled Senate to fill the next Supreme Court vacancy with an opponent of abortion.

The multifront campaign, which begins with a budget of $2 million, will start on Tuesday with television advertising in Washington. It is expected to spread to other cities throughout the fall. As part of the effort, the coalition plans to encourage thousands of abortion opponents to mail baby rattles to their senators.

The campaign comes amid the first signs of stress in the relationship between Mr. Bush and the social conservative movement, an important component of the president's political base.

Mr. Bush's decision last month to allow federal financing for limited stem cell research was supported, or at least condoned, by many social conservatives who might have been expected to oppose it. Those in favor included the National Right to Life Committee, the Rev. Jerry Falwell and James Dobson, president of Focus on the Family. But it was harshly criticized by other groups, including many Roman Catholic and evangelical organizations that maintain there can be no compromise of principles involving the sanctity of life.

The conservative divide on the stem cell issue — essentially between purists and pragmatists — has worried movement strategists who know from experience that they face complacency when a Republican occupies the White House. With the conservative disunity apparent, and with Democrats controlling the Senate, the strategists believe it is vitally important to demonstrate that social conservatives will be unified and aggressive, particularly when it comes to the Supreme Court and abortion.

The organizer of the Shake the Nation campaign, Janet L. Folger, said she hoped it would give Mr. Bush "a lot more confidence and the members of the Senate a lot more courage." She added: "I can tell you this. There can never be another David Souter."

Ms. Folger was referring to the Supreme Court justice appointed by Mr. Bush's father in 1990. Mr. Souter's views on abortion were largely unknown then, and he has disheartened conservatives by voting to protect abortion rights.

Interviews with more than a dozen leaders of social conservative groups suggest that some opponents of the stem cell measure were so alienated by the president's decision that he may have trouble regaining their confidence. That, they said, is a potential problem for a president who lost the popular vote in the 2000 campaign while barely winning the electoral vote.

Paul M. Weyrich, a longtime conservative activist and writer, said he had received more hate mail in response to a commentary in support of Mr. Bush's decision than he had about all of the nearly daily messages he has written over eight years. Mr. Weyrich estimated that perhaps a fourth of social conservatives opposed the stem cell decision.

"When passions run that deeply," Mr. Weyrich said, "I think he's going to have a hard time getting that quarter of the movement back. Maybe he can afford to lose them, but the last election was pretty close. He can't be squishy in the future."

At the very least, Mr. Weyrich and other conservative leaders said, Mr. Bush may have expended much of the political capital he held with social conservatives. And both supporters and opponents of the stem cell decision said they would now be watching attentively as Mr. Bush turns to judicial appointments, education policy and his proposal to allow religious charities to receive expanded federal financing.

"In the final analysis, people are going to be more circumspect," said Kenneth L. Connor, president of the Family Research Council, a public policy group that takes conservative stands on family issues. "The question is, Can the president be counted on or not?"

Karl Rove, the president's top political adviser, said he felt that Mr. Bush's position with his base remained secure.

"There is no group of the president's supporters, other than his family and friends, that is going to support him 100 percent of the time," Mr. Rove said. "But I will say that we were gratified by the level of support from unexpected quarters by people that you might have thought would have been critical of the president's approach."

Social conservatives have made it clear that there is no more important political battleground for them than the Supreme Court, where abortion rights have been affirmed over the last decade by narrow majorities.

While there is no vacancy on the court, three justices — Chief Justice William H. Rehnquist and Justices John Paul Stevens and Sandra Day O'Connor — are over 70. Many court watchers expect at least one retirement within the next few years.

Mr. Bush opposes legalized abortion and has said that he considers the 1973 Roe v. Wade decision to have been a "judicial reach." Justices Stevens and O'Connor have voted to uphold the Roe decision, while the chief justice opposes it.

Mr. Bush said repeatedly during last year's campaign that while he would not apply anti-abortion litmus tests to his judicial appointments, he would look for justices who strictly interpret the Constitution and who do not legislate from the bench.

But at the moment, Mr. Bush would also face the political reality of having to nominate someone capable of winning confirmation from a Senate where Democrats hold a 50-to-49 advantage.

Ms. Folger and her allies hope to ensure that Mr. Bush does not compromise his anti-abortion principles in pursuit of an easy confirmation.

"I don't believe because George Bush is in the White House that it ensures victory," she said. "But it gives us a chance."

Some 23 groups, including the Southern Baptist Convention's Ethics and Religious Liberty Commission, Phyllis Schlafly's Eagle Forum and Charles W. Colson's Prison Fellowship, are participating in the campaign organized by Ms. Folger. Though the campaign was conceived before the stem cell decision was made, many participants said the need to show unity and firmness had been reinforced by that debate.

Ms. Folger is national director of the Center for Reclaiming America, which is affiliated with Coral Ridge Ministries, a group in Fort Lauderdale, Fla., led by the Rev. D. James Kennedy, a pastor with the socially conservative Presbyterian Church of America. The "Shake the Nation" campaign, Ms. Folger said, was inspired in part by a previous coalition effort called "Truth in Love" that encouraged homosexuals to change their sexual orientation.

The campaign's first television advertisement depicts babies dancing and shaking rattles on the Mall in Washington. When a gavel falls announcing the Supreme Court's approval of abortion rights, the babies disappear from the screen. The advertisement closes with a child's voice saying, "Tell your senator to shake the nation back to life."

Mr. Bush began his tenure with tremendous good will from social conservatives, many of whom felt like pariahs during the Clinton administration. Since then, the relationship has been tended dutifully by Mr. Rove and others in the White House who maintain regular contact with movement leaders. On the day Mr. Bush announced his stem cell decision, Mr. Rove placed numerous calls seeking support from prominent conservatives, one of whom he tracked down in the hospital.

Deal W. Hudson, the editor and publisher of Crisis, a conservative Catholic monthly, said that the level of White House access for Catholic leaders "has been historic."

Mr. Hudson, who is in regular contact with Mr. Rove, said the relationship between Mr. Bush and social conservatives remained sound. "You'd really have to be kind of a fanatical one-issue person or group to fall out of the coalition," he said. "Right now there are some who have spoken and are speaking pretty loudly, but I think that will calm down once it's clear the president is not going to let this decision slide down the slippery slope."

That, of course, is the great fear of many conservatives. Many of those interviewed said they would be watching to see whether Mr. Bush responded to pressure from scientists to loosen his restrictions on financing research on stem cells, which he limited to those already extracted from embryos.

In addition to closely studying his judicial appointments, they said they would look for Mr. Bush to renew the fight to allow parents to use taxpayer-financed tuition aid to send children to private schools. They also will pay close attention to whether he defends his ban on federal money for international family planning agencies that perform or promote abortions, and whether he supports religious charities that want to receive federal financing while maintaining their right to not hire homosexuals.

"On a variety of other issues we'll be even more attentive for what will be expectations of a Bush compromise," said Richard Cizik, vice president for governmental affairs of the National Association of Evangelicals. "It's obvious we have to keep the heat on or they won't take us seriously."

Anthrax Scare Hits Groups Backing Right to Abortion

BY TAMAR LEWIN | NOV. 9, 2001

IN THE SECOND WAVE of anthrax threats against abortion clinics in the last month, about 200 clinics and abortion rights groups were sent Federal Express packages containing a powdery substance and, in some cases, a letter signed by the Army of God indicating that the substance was anthrax.

The packages, some of which were delivered yesterday, falsely purported to have come from individuals associated with Planned Parenthood Federation of America or the National Abortion Federation and listed addresses that were close to — but not precisely — those of the advocacy groups.

Eleanor Smeal, the president of the Feminist Majority Foundation, said, "This is the first time we've had an anthrax threat — at least we hope it's just a threat — coming in a FedEx package, and it's an escalation, since they targeted not only the clinics but the advocacy groups like us and Catholics for a Free Choice." Ms. Smeal said she believed that only about 10 of the packages had been opened. So far, she said, the packages have been traced to three sites in Virginia, one in Philadelphia and one in Detroit. She said test results on the powder were not expected until at least today.

Because there have been so many anthrax threats against abortion clinics in the last three years, abortion rights groups have developed routines for notifying all clinics of the threats that have been received, and most are careful to screen their mail.

"We got the first call from a clinic owner in Orlando around 9 o'clock this morning, and immediately put out an alert to all the clinics," Ms. Smeal said. "I don't think too many of the packages got opened."

The F.B.I., which met with Ms. Smeal's group, Planned Parenthood and the National Abortion Federation after a round of anthrax threats last month, has started a nationwide investigation into threats against abortion clinics.

"There definitely seems to be some connection between these packages and the earlier threats," said Stephanie Mueller, a spokeswoman for the National Abortion Federation in Washington. "Some of them said, 'You've ignored our earlier warning. This is the real thing.' "

Ms. Mueller's group received a bomb threat yesterday morning, shortly after the first calls about the anthrax packages arrived, and the building was evacuated for more than an hour.

A spokeswoman for Federal Express said the company was working closely with law enforcement authorities and those affected by the mailings and had identified — and not delivered — "quite a few" of the packages.

"We are investigating these and have found that at least a portion of them were left in drop boxes rather than brought to an individual for delivery," the spokeswoman said.

She added that it was too early to say whether Federal Express would change any procedures for the drop boxes or for charging shipments to third-party accounts.

Who Can Choose?

REVIEW | BY EYAL PRESS | FEB. 3, 2002

BEGGARS AND CHOOSERS

How the Politics of Choice Shapes Adoption,
Abortion, and Welfare in the United States.
By Rickie Solinger.
290 pp. New York:
Hill & Wang. $25.

IN "BEGGARS AND CHOOSERS," Rickie Solinger takes liberals and feminists to task for championing the notion of "choice." This would not be
unusual if she were a conservative who harbors misgivings about the
expansion of women's reproductive options. But she is nothing of the
sort. A historian whose previous books include "Wake Up Little Susie:
Single Pregnancy and Race Before Roe v. Wade," a caustic examination of the limited alternatives available to pregnant women in the
1950's, Solinger is an ardent advocate of women's rights.

Solinger argues here that framing issues like abortion as a matter
of choice is a mistake — not because it affords women too much freedom, but because it does not guarantee them enough: "The contempo-
rary language of choice promises dignity and reproductive autonomy
to women with resources. For women without, the language of choice
is a taunt and a threat." In Solinger's view, the word choice has trans-
formed what ought to be considered a universal right into "a consum-
er's privilege" that only affluent women enjoy.

Although her polemical style may turn off some readers, Solinger
sheds light on several important disparities. For many poor women,
she points out, access to abortions has been severely limited since
1976, when Congress first passed legislation barring Medicaid from
paying for them. Paradoxically, Solinger notes, the cutoff came just
as politicians began proposing punitive measures, like caps on welfare benefits to mothers who bore more children, to prevent depen-
dent women from having too many babies. Solinger concludes that

motherhood itself has become a "class privilege" in America, with poor women stigmatized as "bad" choice-makers whose reproductive lives must be controlled.

Solinger is on to something: if having an abortion is merely a matter of personal preference, the government is under no obligation to make it universally available (a policy that disproportionately impacts the poor). Too often, however, Solinger's fixation on the limits of choice leads her to simplify issues that are enormously complex. Consider her analysis of adoption, which Solinger portrays as an inherently coercive transaction in which wealthy women " 'choose' to become mothers by exploiting the resourcelessness of other women." Adoption does often involve the transfer of children from poor women to comparatively privileged families. But for many pregnant women unable to support families, adoption may be the best available option, just as it may expand the opportunities of women who are infertile (not to mention gay couples who want to raise children).

Another problem is political. While Solinger repeatedly chides feminists for employing the market-friendly language of choice rather than the bolder rhetoric of rights, she never considers the strategic advantages of this approach. As the journalist William Saletan has pointed out, in the mid-1980's abortion proponents made a conscious decision to portray their cause as an effort to preserve individual choice against government encroachment. Talk of women's rights was muted, as advocates focused on courting voters who might oppose abortion but who also oppose state intervention in the personal realm. The strategy did come at a cost, diverting attention from issues like access and equality. But it also enabled politicians favoring abortion rights to reach out to a broader constituency while throwing their critics on the defensive.

Even politicians who fervently oppose abortion rarely talk openly about overturning Roe v. Wade these days. The reason is that in a country where few things are valued more than personal liberty, advocates of abortion rights have managed to link their cause to the notion of individual sovereignty — and to cast their opponents as enemies not only of "women's rights" (a label some defenders of traditional values might welcome) but of "choice."

EYAL PRESS is a senior correspondent at The American Prospect.

Posturing on Abortion

EDITORIAL | BY THE NEW YORK TIMES | APRIL 19, 2002

IN RECENT YEARS, opponents of women's reproductive freedom have come up with increasingly creative schemes to curb abortion rights. One of the newest and most deceptive of these, the egregiously mislabeled Child Custody Protection Act, won easy approval in the House on Wednesday. Far from protecting vulnerable minors, the measure's actual result would be to endanger the lives of desperate young women seeking abortions by denying them assistance from their grandparents or other trusted adults.

Indeed, the legislation's overarching purpose is to reduce young women's access to safe, constitutionally protected abortion services. To that end, it would make it a crime for anyone other than a parent to accompany a minor seeking an abortion across state lines — if the minor has not met her home state's requirements for parental consent.

Beyond flouting the right to reproductive choice established in Roe v. Wade, the bill violates basic principles of federalism and state sovereignty that its Republican backers supposedly hold dear by effectively extending the reach of strict parental notification laws that are on the books in 23 states into the 27 other states.

In an ideal world, pregnant teenagers would always consult with one or both parents before making the difficult decision to seek an abortion. But Congress cannot mandate open family communication, and it is downright dangerous to try. All too often teenagers who do not inform their parents about a pregnancy are victims of physical or sexual abuse within the family, and have good reason to feel afraid. Retaining an attorney to seek a judge's permission to bypass a parental notification rule is not a realistic option for most youngsters.

This is the third time the House has given its blessing to this misguided proposal. But on the other two occasions there was a Democratic president in the White House ready to use his veto pen had the Senate failed to block the bill. Not so now, which makes it crucial that the Senate majority leader, Tom Daschle, rally his pro-choice colleagues to keep the anti-abortion measure from reaching President Bush's desk — and keep grandmothers out of prison.

Advocates Shun 'Pro-Choice' to Expand Message

BY JACKIE CALMES | JULY 28, 2014

WASHINGTON — For all the talk about women's issues in this year's midterm election campaigns, something is missing. One of the most enduring labels of modern politics — pro-choice — has fallen from favor, a victim of changed times and generational preferences.

That shift might seem surprising in this political season, when there has been a renewed focus on reproductive issues like access to abortion and birth control. Yet advocates say that the term pro-choice, which has for so long been closely identified with abortion, does not reflect the range of women's health and economic issues now being debated.

Nor, they add, does it speak to a new generation of young women, who tell pollsters that they reject political labels — not least one that dates back four decades, to the Supreme Court's Roe v. Wade decision that established a constitutional right to abortion.

"The labels we've always used about pro-choice and pro-life — they're outdated and they don't mean anything," said Janet Colm, 62, president of Planned Parenthood Action Fund of Central North Carolina, as she prepared to take several younger women to a summer protest at the legislature in Raleigh. "I used to be a one-issue voter" — pro-choice — "but I think most younger people today aren't."

No pithy phrase has replaced pro-choice. Activists talk mainly of "women's health" and "economic security," usually with policy specifics.

"You just have to take more words," said Dawn Laguens, the executive vice president of the political-advocacy arm of Planned Parenthood and an early proponent of a broader message.

Anti-abortion activists have noticed that their opponents have all but stopped saying pro-choice, and they count that as a victory.

"I find it very encouraging that they find that after 40 years they have to do something different because they know it's not working," said Carol Tobias, the president of the National Right to Life Committee.

Just as longtime activists and historians of the abortion movement cannot cite a moment when pro-choice became advocates' preferred label, current leaders of women's organizations cannot pinpoint when it began losing popularity. It has been gradual, they say, prompted by politics and poll findings back to 2010, the year President Obama's Affordable Care Act became law and Republicans subsequently made gains in Congress and state capitals. Since then Republicans have spent a good deal of energy attacking the law, its birth control mandate, Planned Parenthood and Democrats' economic agenda for women.

The change "is something that we have been talking about for several years," said Cecile Richards, the president of Planned Parenthood Federation of America. "I just think the 'pro-choice' language doesn't really resonate particularly with a lot of young women voters. We're really trying to focus on, what are the real things you're going to lose? Sometimes that's rights. Sometimes that's economic or access to health care for you or for your kids."

Pro-choice became commonplace after the 1973 Roe ruling, to counter the pro-life label of the anti-abortion movement. The description was seen as having broader appeal than "pro-abortion," since it fit those who were personally against abortion but opposed any government control over women's health decisions.

" 'Choice' has been extraordinarily successful as a frame for the abortion-rights side because a lot of Americans may not like the idea of abortion but they definitely agree with the idea of choice," said Suzanne Staggenborg, a professor at the University of Pittsburgh who researches social movements. "And they agree that it should be a woman's choice in consultation with her doctor."

But by 2010 some abortion-rights activists began to sense in their outreach to young women, whose support was needed not only for the midterm elections but for the movement's future as well, that the term pro-choice was virtually meaningless. That was confirmed by post-election polls and focus groups that women's organizations and Democrats commissioned to understand what went wrong.

Among the findings, according to several people familiar with them: Many young women, when asked whether they were pro-choice or pro-life, said pro-life. Yet they supported the Roe ruling. Explaining the contradiction, Ms. Laguens said these self-described pro-life voters were "talking about their personal decision-making, for themselves, and not about what they want to push on others."

But such results also showed the weakness of the pro-choice label, advocates and pollsters said. Planned Parenthood took the lead, conducting research on public attitudes throughout 2011 and then presenting the findings to allies in various meetings.

"It definitely was a bit destabilizing when we started," Ms. Laguens said. When Planned Parenthood produced a YouTube video last year for supporters on the shift to a broader message, one member wrote online: "I'm pro-choice and I won't be bullied into saying anything different. This is nothing but a retreat and a shame!"

Representative Louise M. Slaughter, Democrat of New York, who for 15 years has been a co-chairwoman of the Pro-Choice Caucus in Congress, scoffed at the idea of a name change. "I've never worried about it," she said.

Emily's List, a political fund-raising organization formed three decades ago to back female candidates who support abortion rights, still says on its website's home page, "We ignite change by getting pro-choice Democratic women elected to office." But its research arm, American Women, like Planned Parenthood, has also done extensive polling and recently produced a "tool kit" for candidates and activists — customized for each state — of economic policies for women, including paid leave, higher minimum wage, equal pay for women and men for equivalent work, and birth control coverage. ("Birth control is only a social issue if you've never had to pay for it," advocates often say, to highlight the economic angle.)

The broadened message from women's groups coincided with — and, they say, was hastened by — Republicans' actions after taking control of the House and some state legislatures in the 2010 elections. Congressional Republicans sought to defund Planned Parenthood, threatening a government shutdown. Then they began their campaign to repeal the Affordable Care Act, which includes specific benefits for women — mandated coverage of contraception, mammograms and annual gynecological exams without co-payments; an end to an insurance industry rating system that charged women more than men, and a ban on insurers refusing to cover people with pre-existing conditions.

Republicans singled out the birth control benefit of the Affordable Care Act as a violation of employers' religious freedom. They proposed "personhood" amendments defining life as starting at conception, which would criminalize not only abortion but also some fertility treatments. And they blocked economic proposals like equal pay.

"When you really look at the broad scope of all the Republicans' attacks," said Marcy Stech, a spokeswoman for Emily's List, "it's clear 'women's health' is what's at stake."

Where the Pro-Life Movement Goes Next

OPINION | BY MARY ZIEGLER | JULY 2, 2016

FOR THE PRO-LIFE MOVEMENT, the Supreme Court's decision on Monday in two Texas abortion regulations was the most devastating defeat in decades. Representative Chris Smith, a New Jersey Republican who is one of the movement's most vocal supporters, described the decision as "tragic," irrefutable proof of "the incredibly high stakes the Supreme Court vacancy holds for the unborn child."

The sting of the defeat in this case, Whole Woman's Health v. Hellerstedt, is hard to overstate. It puts teeth in the "undue burden" test, the standard applied to abortion regulations since 1992. That test makes it unconstitutional for a state regulation to place "a substantial obstacle in the path of a woman seeking an abortion." Until now, though, legal experts had disagreed about exactly what the test meant.

Now, the court has said that if the law doesn't serve any real health purpose — as it found with Texas's regulation of hospital admitting privileges and clinic requirements — it could fail the test.

Politically, the decision in the Texas case also stopped cold the momentum of what had seemed to be a promising strategy of focusing on women, and laws that legislators said protected women against dangerous conditions in abortion clinics.

Texas' emphasis on protecting women once made sense as part of a much larger anti-abortion campaign. In the 1990s, pro-lifers recognized that the movement had an image problem. While Americans saw abortion opponents as morally principled, polls showed that the public also sometimes viewed them as cold, indifferent or even extremist in their attitudes toward women. But the tactic at play in Hellerstedt put women first. As a movement pamphlet put it: "Once average citizens realize that women are being hurt by abortion, they will begin to question why we allow abortion at all."

So where do abortion opponents go from here?

Pro-lifers have to decide if a legal strategy focused on women is one they want to stick with — and if the political party to which they have tied their fortunes still deserves their support. In the past decade, the movement's success has mostly concealed activists' sometimes clashing views about strategy. Now, with a major legal setback, the movement risks fracturing again.

Finding a perfect historical comparison is hard, but the best understood pro-life setback came in 1973, when the Supreme Court decided Roe v. Wade. That case invalidated the vast majority of criminal abortion laws in the nation and left the states little room to regulate abortion early in pregnancy.

After Roe, pro-lifers concentrated more than ever on arguing for the rights of the unborn, but movement members disagreed about strategy. Some gave up on litigation, and focused on amending the Constitution, believing that the court had deliberately disregarded the rights of the unborn.

Dr. William Colliton, a veteran movement member, spoke for many who believed that the Supreme Court had already "evaded the scientific answer to the question, 'When does life begin?' " so pressing on that point was futile. Others responded that the problem was ignorance. If the American public was educated about "what is really done to that living being, the child in the womb, they will reject abortion on demand," argued Americans United for Life.

The Texas decision forces the movement into a comparable debate. Some members have already suggested that it is time to refocus on fetal rights.

Others suggest that strategies focused on women still have untapped potential. The conservative magazine National Review argued that pro-lifers had won in the Supreme Court when they introduced narrower versions of legislation and collected better proof to support it.

Now as before, movement members will have to decide whether to prove that abortion really hurts women or turn more exclusively to arguments about fetal rights.

The decision on the Texas cases also finds the pro-life movement in a familiar debate about the wisdom of relying on the Republican Party. After Roe, when it became clear that Congress would not amend the Constitution to ban abortion, some pro-lifers prioritized the incremental attack still at work today. As part of this strategy, abortion opponents channeled considerable resources into electoral politics. "Abortion came to us through the law," Dr. John Willke of the National Right to Life Committee wrote his colleagues about the strategy. "Lawmakers make laws. Lawmakers appoint judges. We elect lawmakers. Someday we will again forbid abortion by changing the law."

After political realignment, the Republican Party seemed to be the only logical ally in this effort. By 1984, Dr. Willke seemed almost surprised by questions about which party pro-lifers would choose at the polls. "The choice is very clear-cut," he said. "It is Mr. Reagan."

For others, particularly movement absolutists, relying too much on the Republican Party seemed foolish. These activists believed that politicians would sell out the movement when it was expedient to do so.

Donald J. Trump's candidacy has reopened this schism. Mr. Trump has a record that is anything but pro-life. In March, he seemed open to punishing women who had abortions — the closest thing to apostasy in pro-life circles. After the Texas decision, he again raised concerns by taking almost a week to comment on the case.

The alternative to Mr. Trump for pro-lifers is not obvious. However, the movement's partnership with Republicans has been neither inevitable nor universally accepted. Immediately after Roe, many abortion opponents gravitated toward the Democratic Party, identifying their cause with liberals' fight for civil rights for minority groups.

After the movement joined with Republicans, groups like Democrats for Life have resisted dependence on a single party. Now, more abortion opponents might follow suit. They could also spend time and money more heavily on state and local races. State legislatures have been the most reliable source of anti-abortion legislation for decades.

Whatever abortion opponents choose to do next, Mr. Trump's rise makes reliance on the political status quo seem unwise. Abortion opponents rejoiced after Justice Anthony M. Kennedy, nominated by Ronald Reagan, took his place on the Supreme Court. After the Texas decision, movement members would do well to remember how that turned out.

MARY ZIEGLER is a professor of law at Florida State University and the author of "After Roe: The Lost History of the Abortion Debate."

CHAPTER 4

The Uncertain Future of U.S. Abortion Rights

As justices have retired or passed away and been replaced on the Supreme Court under the Trump administration, there have been concerns that Roe v. Wade could be overturned by an increasingly conservative Court. Medical advances have made abortion services much safer, but state legislation is key to ensuring access to those services. Socially, the debate between advocates and opponents is as robust as ever, brimming with questions on the ethical, religious and health implications of abortion.

Roe v. Wade Was About More Than Abortion

OPINION | BY MARY ZIEGLER | JAN. 21, 2018

THE EVENTS PLANNED to mark the 45th anniversary of Roe v. Wade have one main thing in common: They focus on abortion. In protesting Roe this year, March for Life celebrated a record low abortion rate, proclaiming that "love saves lives." California lawmakers introduced a resolution last year describing Roe as "the cornerstone of women's ability to control their reproductive lives."

But as the nation again considers the legacy of the country's best-known Supreme Court decision, issued on Jan. 22, 1973, we have mostly forgotten part of the story of Roe v. Wade — one almost entirely disconnected from abortion. In the 1970s and beyond, Americans used Roe to answer much larger questions: What does the right to privacy mean, and who can claim that right?

Because we so often identify Roe with a woman's right to choose, we forget that the original decision attracted the ire of feminists who believed that the court had focused too little on women's interests in fertility control. The court held that the right to privacy was broad enough to encompass a woman's decision, with her doctor, to terminate her pregnancy. The justices also reasoned that the government's interest in protecting fetal life did not become compelling until the point of viability.

But why wield the court's decision as a weapon for social change? Most scholars agreed that Roe was a poorly reasoned opinion. What was the appeal for grass-roots activists?

The answer is that Roe's definition of privacy seemed different. More than other Supreme Court decisions, it connected privacy to ideas about individual identity and choice. Whatever the flaws of the original decision, many hoped to use it to redefine who was thought to have autonomy and why.

Civil libertarians, feminists and supporters of L.G.B.T. rights argued that the right to privacy stated in the abortion decision covered other decisions about sexual intimacy. The American Civil Liberties Union used Roe in defending sex workers, gays and lesbians, porn stars and women cohabiting with their boyfriends.

Conservatives as well as liberals invoked this newly articulated right to privacy. With the spread of computers, politicians like Barry Goldwater and his son, the former Republican representative Barry Goldwater Jr., pointed to Roe in demanding privacy protections for personal information.

Champions of consumers' rights read the abortion decision as suggesting that patients could choose any course of treatment, including unproven alternative remedies. Those seeking a right to die used it in the fight for autonomy at the end of life.

For more than a decade, Roe appealed to different groups exploring the untapped potential of the right to privacy. People on both the right and the left saw possible connections between privacy and individual interests in conscientious objection, self-determination and equal treatment.

So how did one decision 45 years ago become synonymous with abortion and nothing else? In part, other privacy fights fizzled when the coalitions backing new rights collapsed. Feminists and libertarians clashed about the line between sexual coercion and sexual privacy. Those who hoped to expand data privacy disagreed about when the government had a good enough reason to collect personal data.

Abortion foes and Republican politicians consciously tried to redefine Roe, equating the decision with abortion and judicial activism. Ronald Reagan had to assure social conservatives that he would pick federal judges who opposed abortion, but he also consistently promised to select nominees based on their accomplishments and judicial philosophy. Labeling Roe an activist decision helped Reagan and other Republicans strike this balance.

Abortion opponents initially did not take much interest in arguments about judicial activism, seeing them as a distraction from the fight for an amendment that would ban all abortions. But by the 1980s, it was obvious that a fetal rights amendment would not pass soon. Delegitimizing Roe suddenly seemed an important step toward the movement's new goal of overruling the 1973 decision.

On Roe's 45th anniversary, we should stop to think about where the right to privacy stands today. The picture does not seem very rosy. Since the new year, there have been fresh concerns about data breaches and the misuse of digital information by giants like Facebook and Google. Privacy and conscience have taken center stage as the Supreme Court considers whether a Christian baker can refuse to serve a same-sex couple. It is easy to believe that the right to privacy is ineffective, more likely to shore up a dissatisfying status quo.

But part of Roe's legacy is the many ways conservatives and liberals once reimagined the right to privacy. Social movements hardly felt constrained by what the Supreme Court had written.

Some pointed to privacy not just in asking for freedom from the government but also in demanding financial support from the state. Others asked not just to be left alone behind closed doors but also to get respect for relationships in public. People tried to use the right to privacy to transform attitudes about sexuality, death and the collection of digital data.

Americans have rethought the right to privacy before. There is no reason we couldn't do it again.

MARY ZIEGLER is a professor of law at Florida State University and the author of "Beyond Abortion: Roe v. Wade and the Battle for Privacy."

How to Talk About Abortion

OPINION | BY LAURIE SHRAGE | MARCH 19, 2018

WHEN MORAL PHILOSOPHERS and others take up an issue that is at the center of public debate, we tend to frame it as a matter of individual ethics. Is it morally permissible to eat meat? To offer money for sex? To have an abortion? Yet, such questions often fail to focus on the issues that are important and relevant for public policy and, as a result, can derail productive public debate.

The problem is that questions like these oversimplify the issues. Consider, for instance, that "abortion" is really an umbrella term for a number of different medical procedures — appropriate for different stages of pregnancy — each with significantly different health risks. Abortion is first and foremost a medical service or procedure, not an individual action, and thus a more important and relevant question for public policy is, Under what circumstances, or for what reasons, should a government prohibit properly trained medical professionals from performing an abortion? This is a question that fellow citizens can productively debate, and that may lead to a consensus.

The relevant public policy question raises issues of medical privacy, limits on governmental power, and the protection of public health, all of which as citizens we need to debate as a matter of social ethics and political values. The individual or personal ethics question — on the moral acceptability of abortion — is not likely to generate a public consensus, given the current lack of agreement on many background issues.

It is well known that members of our society hold vastly different views about when personhood or a human life begins, about our moral obligations to our genetic offspring, or what kind of sexual acts are permissible. That is to be expected. A pluralist, democratic society can accommodate a good amount of such disagreement. Yet it is necessary that we do reach a strong consensus about how to regulate a public

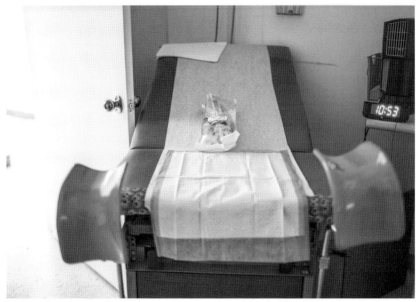

Supplies for the following day's abortions are laid out in one of the rooms of an abortion clinic in Montgomery, Ala.

service, and so moral, political and philosophical analyses should aim to illuminate the issues that can help generate such a consensus.

This should be the case not only for abortion. For example, to productively discuss the opioid abuse crisis, we should ask how our government should regulate doctors who prescribe opioids or pharmacies that distribute them, not when is it morally permissible for an individual to take an opioid (or any addictive) drug. The marriage equality movement raised the question of whether our government should recognize marriages between two people of the same sex, not whether those marriages are ethical. Public debate on this question over the past few decades has been productive and illuminating.

So what about abortion? How should governments restrict or regulate the abortion services offered by medical professionals or facilities? Because this is an issue about good medicine, we need to focus on health risks and outcomes instead of personal ethics. There is broad agreement that medical professionals and facilities should be able to offer services or remedies that are lifesaving and health-preserving for their patients, and they should be prohibited from doing so when the health risks of those services outweigh their health benefits. Given what we now know about the safety of abortion procedures at different stages of pregnancy, and the risks posed by pregnancy and childbirth, what justifications can be offered for restricting abortion services?

It is true that abortion procedures commonly used a century ago were highly dangerous for patients. With advances in medicine, though, the procedures in use today pose fewer risks to a woman's life or health than pregnancy or childbirth itself. A 2012 study of abortion in the United States published in the journal Obstetrics & Gynecology, concluded: "Legal induced abortion is markedly safer than childbirth. The risk of death associated with childbirth is approximately 14 times higher than that with abortion."

There is a lot packed into that statistic, but we often forget that pregnancy and childbirth pose health risks, which vary for women depending on their age, health status, projected need for a cesarean section, number of previous pregnancies and the spacing between them, and so on. Given these risks, access to legal abortion is, in general, life- and health-preserving for women. Our public debates need to consider the state's interest in protecting women's health and the limits of state power in interfering with the decisions we make about how best to preserve our own health or protect our own lives.

A recent report by the National Academies of Sciences, Engineering and Medicine concludes that "The clinical evidence clearly shows that legal abortions in the United States — whether by medication, aspiration, D & E, or induction — are safe and effective. Serious complications are rare. But the risks of serious complication increases with weeks' gestation." This means that state laws and policies that unnecessarily delay the scheduling of an abortion procedure hinder, rather than help, the government in pursuing its interest in protecting women's health.

The state also has an interest in protecting fetal human life, even if fetuses are not legal persons, but this state interest needs to be balanced against others. Nevertheless, our courts have determined repeatedly that, until the last third or so of a pregnancy, the state's interest in protecting women's health and decisional privacy outweighs its interest in protecting fetal life. Yet, why do these interests need to be rebalanced in the last part of pregnancy?

First, performing an abortion in the last months of pregnancy is medically more complicated and poses a higher degree of risk than one performed earlier. Moreover, a pregnant woman in the late stages of a healthy pregnancy has already endured most of the bodily burdens of a pregnancy, and thus the health benefits of an abortion at that stage may not outweigh the risks.

Second, given the viability of the fetus in the late stages of pregnancy, an abortion — a medical procedure in which the fetus's death is an unavoidable outcome — imposes on the medical staff the act of performing a procedure in which a viable fetus will die. It is only reasonable to order a medical team to do this when such a procedure is medically necessary. Alternatively, attempting to induce a premature live birth that is not medically necessary, should a woman request this, would likely injure a viable fetus and endanger its postnatal health and life. Because an abortion is a medical service, and not something a woman decides or does by herself, her right to decisional privacy in this matter is not absolute.

Given these considerations, governments have a compelling interest in restricting abortions in late stages of a healthy pregnancy, but they have an equally compelling interest in ensuring that legal and safe abortions are available to women, without burdensome restrictions, before the last third or so of a pregnancy.

If, in the future, a public consensus on the question of when human personhood begins (in particular, one that agrees that a human person could exist before any complex psychological properties have developed), then we would need to recognize that there is more than one "patient" involved in an abortion. We are not there yet. To get there, the minority who believe this would have to convince the rest of us of this metaphysical, or religiously based, assertion. Until they do, we need to focus on the more manageable and relevant question of how to regulate a medical service or procedure that is sought by millions of women.

When there is a lack of public consensus on a moral question, our public policies need to reflect the principles on which there is broad agreement. In a liberal democracy, we don't need to resolve many difficult questions of individual morality in order to have defensible public policies — policies that are justified by our commitment to democratic decision making, liberty and equality. State officials who appeal to their own beliefs on questions of individual morality, in order to justify their policy decisions, are violating values more fundamental to our society.

Questions like "Is homosexuality immoral?" or "Is abortion immoral?" suggest that entire groups of people that pursue activities necessary to securing their basic human needs are possibly morally compromised, and are thus insulting; they also encourage civic leaders and their constituents to take up rigid and extreme views based on their own personal convictions, and to be morally arrogant toward others who don't share their views.

Raising these questions in the midst of heated public debate about access to abortion services or to civil marriage makes it seem as if we are hopelessly divided as a society in ways that render the policy questions irresolvable. Yet questions about individual moral behavior or personal ethics, which still generate wide disagreement based on religious diversity, are not really all that relevant to the issue of lawmaking. In short, what a good society does is based on a different set of considerations and principles than what a good person does.

LAURIE SHRAGE is the author of "Abortion and Social Responsibility: Depolarizing the Debate" and a professor of philosophy at Florida International University.

Walgreens Pharmacist Denies Woman With Unviable Pregnancy the Medication Needed to End It

BY LOUIS LUCERO II | JUNE 25, 2018

NINE WEEKS INTO her pregnancy, Nicole Arteaga got distressing news from her doctor: There was no fetal heartbeat and the pregnancy would end in a miscarriage.

Rather than have a surgical procedure to remove the fetal tissue from her uterus, Ms. Arteaga, a first-grade teacher who lives in Peoria, Ariz., decided on Wednesday to take misoprostol, a medication that can be used to end a failed pregnancy.

The medication is approved by the federal Food and Drug Administration for use by a licensed provider to end a pregnancy within the first 10 weeks, for what is known as a medical abortion.

She dropped off a prescription for the medication and by that night, got an email saying it was ready to be picked up.

But when she tried to get the medication from her local Walgreens on Thursday, the pharmacist asked whether she was pregnant. When she said she was, he refused to give her the misoprostol, citing "his ethical beliefs," she recalled in a detailed account on Facebook.

Ms. Arteaga described her response in the post, which has been shared more than 30,000 times.

"I stood at the mercy of this pharmacist explaining my situation in front of my 7-year-old, and five customers standing behind only to be denied because of his ethical beliefs," she wrote, adding, "I left Walgreens in tears, ashamed and feeling humiliated by a man who knows nothing of my struggles but feels it is his right to deny medication prescribed to me by my doctor."

Walgreens said on Saturday that it had contacted Ms. Arteaga "and apologized for how the situation was handled," but suggested that the employee had not run afoul of company policy by refusing to fill the prescription.

"To respect the sincerely held beliefs of our pharmacists while at the same time meeting the needs of our patients, our policy allows pharmacists to step away from filling a prescription for which they have a moral objection," the company said in a statement.

In an update to her original post, which includes a photo of the pharmacist's business card, Ms. Arteaga said her prescription was ultimately transferred to another Walgreens, where she was able to get the medication "with no problems."

Ms. Arteaga's account evoked strong reactions on social media, where some called on Walgreens to fire the pharmacist and others threatened to boycott the company.

"I was shocked," Ms. Arteaga, 35, said on Sunday. "I couldn't believe that he would tell me that I wasn't going to be able to get my prescription."

She tried to explain her situation but he remained unmoved. "What I have inside of me is an undeveloped baby," she recalled telling the pharmacist. "I need this to help get it out."

In its statement, the drugstore chain said that pharmacists who object to a medication are nonetheless "required to refer the prescription to another pharmacist or manager on duty to meet the patient's needs in a timely manner," and that it was "looking into the matter."

A company spokesman, Jim Graham, declined to explain what the investigation might entail.

Six states — including Arizona — explicitly permit pharmacies or pharmacists to refuse to provide medication because of religious or moral objections, according to the National Women's Law Center, a nonprofit and advocacy group.

Nancy Berlinger, a research scholar at the Hastings Center, an independent bioethics research institution, said that so-called conscience clauses have been established law for years. "This is a very, very well-protected right in the United States," so much so that a principle called duty of care can sometimes be compromised, she said.

"You have a right to step away, but you don't have a right to step between" patients and their access to legal and medically appropriate treatment options, she added.

The name on the business card that Ms. Arteaga photographed, Brian Hreniuc, is included in a directory of licensed pharmacists in Arizona. No one could be reached on Sunday afternoon at a phone number associated with that name.

Ms. Arteaga's post described her anguish over her pregnancy complications — a pain, she suggested, he couldn't possibly empathize with.

"I get it we all have our beliefs," she wrote. "But what he failed to understand is this isn't the situation I had hoped for, this isn't something I wanted. This is something I have zero control over. He has no idea what it's like to want nothing more than to carry a child to full term and be unable to do so."

SARAH MERVOSH contributed reporting.

Supreme Court Backs Anti-Abortion Pregnancy Centers in Free Speech Case

BY ADAM LIPTAK | JUNE 26, 2018

WASHINGTON — Ruling for opponents of abortion on free speech grounds, the Supreme Court said on Tuesday that the State of California may not require religiously oriented "crisis pregnancy centers" to supply women with information about how to end their pregnancies.

The case was a clash between state efforts to provide women with facts about their medical options and First Amendment rulings that place limits on the government's ability to compel people to say things at odds with their beliefs.

Justice Clarence Thomas, writing for the five-justice conservative majority, accepted the free-speech argument, ruling that the First Amendment prohibits California from forcing the centers, which oppose abortion on religious grounds, to post notices about how to obtain the procedure. The centers seek to persuade women to choose parenting or adoption.

"Licensed clinics must provide a government-drafted script about the availability of state-sponsored services, as well as contact information for how to obtain them," Justice Thomas wrote. "One of those services is abortion — the very practice that petitioners are devoted to opposing."

California, he wrote, can use other means to tell women about the availability of abortion, including advertising. But "California cannot co-opt the licensed facilities to deliver its message for it," he wrote.

The case was the first touching on abortion since Justice Neil M. Gorsuch, who sided with the majority, joined the court. While the decision's legal analysis turned on the First Amendment, it was lost on no one that the justices most committed to defending abortion rights were all in dissent.

The court returned the case to the lower courts for another look, but it seemed unlikely that California would be able to present new evidence or arguments to save the law.

In a dissent that he summarized from the bench, Justice Stephen G. Breyer accused the majority of acting inconsistently. In 1992, he noted, the Supreme Court upheld a Pennsylvania law that required doctors who performed abortions to provide some kinds of information to their patients.

"If a state can lawfully require a doctor to tell a woman seeking an abortion about adoption services, why should it not be able, as here, to require a medical counselor to tell a woman seeking prenatal care or other reproductive health care about childbirth and abortion services?" he asked.

"As the question suggests," Justice Breyer wrote, "there is no convincing reason to distinguish between information about adoption and information about abortion in this context. After all, the rule of law embodies evenhandedness, and 'what is sauce for the goose is normally sauce for the gander.' "

Justice Thomas responded that the 1992 decision was different because it concerned a medical procedure. Justice Breyer was unpersuaded.

"Really?" he asked. "No one doubts that choosing an abortion is a medical procedure that involves certain health risks. But the same is true of carrying a child to term and giving birth."

Chief Justice John G. Roberts Jr. and Justices Gorsuch, Anthony M. Kennedy and Samuel A. Alito Jr. joined the majority opinion.

In a concurring opinion, Justice Kennedy said the First Amendment bars compelling people to betray their beliefs.

"Governments must not be allowed to force persons to express a message contrary to their deepest convictions," he wrote. "Freedom of speech secures freedom of thought and belief. This law imperils those liberties."

Michael P. Farris, a lawyer with Alliance Defending Freedom, which represented the centers, said he welcomed the ruling.

"No one should be forced by the government to express a message that violates their convictions, especially on deeply divisive subjects such as abortion," he said. "In this case, the government used its power to force pro-life pregnancy centers to provide free advertising for abortion. The Supreme Court said that the government can't do that, and that it must respect pro-life beliefs."

California's attorney general, Xavier Becerra, said the ruling would place needless barriers between women and access to medical care.

"When it comes to making their health decisions, all California women — regardless of their economic background or ZIP code — deserve access to critical and nonbiased information to make their own informed decisions," he said.

The case, National Institute of Family and Life Advocates v. Becerra, No. 16-1140, concerned a California law that requires centers operated by opponents of abortion to provide women with information about the availability of the procedure.

The state requires the centers to post notices that free or low-cost abortion, contraception and prenatal care are available to low-income women through public programs, and to provide the phone number for more information.

The centers argued that the law violated their right to free speech by forcing them to convey messages at odds with their beliefs. The law's defenders said the notices combat incomplete or misleading information provided by the clinics.

The California Legislature found that the roughly 200 centers in the state used "intentionally deceptive advertising and counseling practices that often confuse, misinform and even intimidate women from making fully informed, time-sensitive decisions about critical health care."

A separate part of the law applies to unlicensed clinics. They are not required to post notices about the availability of abortion, but are required to disclose that they are not licensed by the state.

Justice Thomas said those requirements, which can require notices in as many as 13 languages, were too burdensome. In dissent, Justice Breyer wrote that the question should have been decided in the context of particular disputes and not as a general matter.

"Whether the requirement of 13 different languages goes too far and is unnecessarily burdensome in light of the need to secure the statutory objectives is a matter that concerns Los Angeles County alone, and it is a proper subject for a Los Angeles-based as-applied challenge in light of whatever facts a plaintiff finds relevant," Justice Breyer wrote. "At most, such facts might show a need for fewer languages, not invalidation of the statute."

Justices Ruth Bader Ginsburg, Sonia Sotomayor and Elena Kagan joined Justice Breyer's dissent.

Tuesday's ruling reversed a unanimous decision from a three-judge panel of the United States Court of Appeals for the Ninth Circuit, in San Francisco, which had upheld both parts of the law.

"California has a substantial interest in the health of its citizens, including ensuring that its citizens have access to and adequate information about constitutionally protected medical services like abortion," Judge Dorothy W. Nelson wrote for the panel in upholding the requirement that licensed clinics post a notice about abortion.

"The notice informs the reader only of the existence of publicly funded family-planning services," Judge Nelson wrote. "It does not contain any more speech than necessary, nor does it encourage, suggest or imply that women should use those state-funded services."

Other federal appeals courts had struck down similar laws, saying that the government could find other ways to inform women about their options.

The Ninth Circuit also upheld the requirement that unlicensed clinics disclose that they are unlicensed.

"California has a compelling interest in informing pregnant women when they are using the medical services of a facility that has not satisfied licensing standards set by the state," Judge Nelson wrote.

"And given the Legislature's findings regarding the existence of" the centers, "which often present misleading information to women about reproductive medical services, California's interest in presenting accurate information about the licensing status of individual clinics is particularly compelling."

Much of Tuesday's decision was a continuation of a debate at the Supreme Court about how courts should analyze First Amendment challenges.

Justice Thomas wrote that laws restricting speech must be subject to searching scrutiny, while Justice Breyer expressed concern that free speech arguments were being used to undermine ordinary and sensible regulations.

"Using the First Amendment to strike down economic and social laws that legislatures long would have thought themselves free to enact will, for the American public, obscure, not clarify, the true value of protecting freedom of speech," Justice Breyer wrote.

Bulwark Against an Abortion Ban? Medical Advances

BY PAM BELLUCK AND JAN HOFFMAN | JULY 1, 2018

AS PARTISANS ON both sides of the abortion divide contemplate a Supreme Court with two Trump appointees, one thing is certain: America even without legal abortion would be very different from America before abortion was legal.

The moment Justice Anthony M. Kennedy announced his retirement, speculation swirled that Roe v. Wade, the landmark 1973 ruling that legalized abortion, would be overturned. Most legal experts say that day is years away, if it arrives at all. A more likely scenario, they predict, is that a rightward-shifting court would uphold efforts to restrict abortion, which would encourage some states to further limit access.

Even then, a full-fledged return to an era of back-alley, coat-hanger abortions seems improbable. In the decades since Roe was decided, a burst of scientific innovation has produced more effective, simpler and safer ways to prevent pregnancies and to stop them after conception — advances that have contributed to an abortion rate that has already plunged by half since the 1980s.

"We're in a new world now," said Aziza Ahmed, a law professor at Northeastern University who writes about reproductive rights law. "The majority of American women are on some form of contraception. We take it for granted that we can control when and how we want to reproduce. We see pregnancy as within the realm that we can control."

Women have powerful tools at hand: improved intrauterine devices and hormonal implants that can prevent pregnancy for years at a time; inexpensive home pregnancy tests able to detect pregnancy very early; and morning-after pills, some even available over the counter, which can prevent pregnancy if taken up to five days after unprotected sex.

Medication abortions enable women up to 10 weeks pregnant to take two pills, the first supervised by a doctor and the second at home, to terminate a pregnancy without surgery. In 2013, nearly a quarter of abortions were accomplished with medication, up from 10 percent in 2004. Even in countries that have banned virtually all abortions, including some in Latin America, women have managed to get these drugs from websites and abortion rights organizations that ship them.

And the Affordable Care Act, which has so far defied repeated repeal attempts, has made birth control available to poor and working-class women, and also to those with private coverage through employers, with its requirement that most insurers cover the full cost of contraception. Apps and telemedicine services are making birth control pills and other methods available without even a visit to a doctor.

Still, legal changes that make abortion less available would have profound effects on millions of women, disproportionately affecting African-Americans, Latinas and women struggling economically. And access to contraception can be problematic for low-income single women in the 19 states, including Texas and Florida, that have still not expanded Medicaid coverage for poor single adults.

Despite the new drugs and technologies, nearly half of all pregnancies in the United States are unintended, a higher rate than in many other developed countries.

A report this year by a committee of the National Academies of Sciences, Engineering and Medicine found that three-quarters of women who have abortions are poor or low-income, and 61 percent are women of color. Such women bear the brunt of state laws that restrict abortion, including those requiring multiple appointments or waiting periods or that limit which providers can perform abortions.

Such hurdles and delays could eventually threaten the consistently high level of safety in abortion procedures, experts said. "We found that more and more regulations on abortion and abortion procedures reduced the quality of care," said the committee's co-chairwoman,

The Spread of State Abortion Restrictions

The Guttmacher Institute rates states based on how many of 10 major abortion restrictions they have in place. Many states, especially in the South and Midwest, had more restrictions in 2017 than in 2000.

Number of major abortion restrictions

0   1   3   5   7   9   10

2000

2017

BY ASH NGU AND SARA SIMON/THE NEW YORK TIMES

Dr. Helene Gayle, president and chief executive of the Chicago Community Trust.

"The people most impacted are the immigrant women already under siege, low-income women, women of color, transgender and queer women," said Jessica González-Rojas, executive director of the National Latina Institute for Reproductive Health, which works with women in the Rio Grande Valley in Texas. "Having a Supreme Court friendly to these restrictive laws makes it a de facto ban on that kind of health care, abortion and contraception. Legal access without real access is not access at all."

In some states, though, the impact of anti-abortion laws can be hard to measure. A recent report on 2014 data by the Guttmacher Institute, a research group that supports abortion rights, found that while the national abortion rate had reached its lowest since the Roe v. Wade decision, the rate rose modestly in six states — five of which had introduced restrictive abortion laws.

The report also found that in states where the number of abortion clinics had increased, women were not necessarily having more abortions. New Jersey went from having 24 clinics in 2011 to 41 in 2014, but abortions declined from about 47,000 to about 44,000 during that time.

Overall, abortion rates have declined almost steadily since 1981, when the rate was 29.3 per 1,000 women. In 2014, there were an estimated 926,200 abortions — a rate of 14.6 per 1,000 women, ages 15 to 44.

BACK WHEN ABORTION WAS BANNED

When abortion was outlawed, initially by state laws in the 19th century, women still managed to obtain them, sometimes with doctors or midwives, sometimes with unlicensed abortionists.

"Making abortions illegal didn't stop them ever," said Linda Gordon, a professor of history at New York University.

The so-called Comstock obscenity laws, passed from 1873 through the early 1900s, made it illegal to give, sell, mail or transport any item used for contraception or abortion.

After that, "Margaret Sanger built a movement by compromising," Dr. Gordon said. "They would campaign for legalization of contraception but not abortion."

Even after the birth control pill went on the market in 1960, contraceptives were only provided to women who were married. "When I was in college, there was a wedding ring that was shared among young women when they wanted to see a doctor to get contraception," Dr. Gordon said.

Abortions were often arranged through networks of clergy or women who helped people find, travel to and pay for providers.

Johanna Schoen, a professor at Rutgers University in New Brunswick, N.J., who specializes in the history of women's reproductive health, said the fate and rate of abortion will be intertwined with the availability of contraception, and whether anti-abortion political forces also take aim at birth control.

Professor Schoen said many European countries have low abortion rates because birth control and sex education are widely available. "But in the United States, the same people who are trying to restrict abortions have tried to restrict contraception, too."

DEATH BY A THOUSAND CUTS?

Carol Sanger, who teaches reproductive rights at Columbia Law School, predicts that the Supreme Court won't overrule Roe v. Wade anytime soon. Developing a case that would be a direct assault takes years, she said.

"You don't say, 'Kennedy's out, Roe's overturned,' " Ms. Sanger said.

The doctrine of precedent, known as stare decisis, "to stand by things decided," is sturdy. Circumstances must be extraordinary, a law unworkable, for a court to overrule itself, Ms. Sanger said. "It stands for the idea that the substance of our law doesn't blow back and forth just because we get a new administration."

Another reason Roe v. Wade may not be struck down? "You can do a heck of a lot of damage without overturning it," she said.

In the 45 years since the ruling, anti-abortion activists have largely focused on lobbying state legislatures for laws that delay or limit access to abortion, including mandating parental notification by teenagers, longer waiting periods, and strict requirements for clinics.

Among such initiatives, said Susan Swayze Liebel of the Susan B. Anthony List, an anti-abortion organization, "fetal pain" laws have become a "top priority." Some 20 states have enacted these laws, which assert that a fetus can feel pain at 20 weeks after conception — a claim refuted by most medical experts.

Roe barred most legal restrictions on abortions until fetuses were considered able to survive outside the womb, believed then to be 24 weeks after a woman's last menstrual period (about 22 weeks after conception). These laws seek to shorten abortion deadlines by two weeks, and while more than 90 percent of abortions occur much earlier, in the first trimester, fetal pain laws serve as potent political rallying cries.

Numerous lawsuits about abortion restrictions are currently in state and federal courts, primed to wound Roe with a thousand cuts.

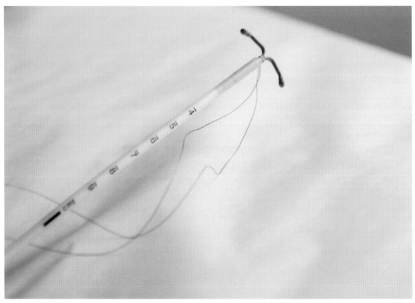

Improved and safer intrauterine devices can prevent pregnancy for years, morning-after pills can prevent pregnancy after unprotected sex, and medication abortions can help women terminate a pregnancy without surgery.

Like the fetal pain laws, the intention of one such category is to roll back viability dates, which goes to the heart of Roe. Iowa just enacted a law banning most abortions after six weeks, when a fetal heartbeat can be detected. Mississippi recently passed a ban on abortions after 15 weeks. Abortion providers swiftly sued after the laws were passed. Legislators who sponsored the laws said they relished such court clashes, hoping to reach the Supreme Court.

Another category is TRAP laws: targeted regulation of abortion providers. An Arkansas law, for example, requires providers of medication abortions to have a contract with an obstetrician/gynecologist with hospital admitting privileges. The Supreme Court declined to consider an appeal by the plaintiffs, Planned Parenthood of Arkansas and Eastern Oklahoma, of an appellate court ruling that upheld the law. The clinics say finding such doctors who will work with them has been impossible. The case is back in federal court, where a judge has blocked the law until July 2. If the law takes effect, Arkansas will likely lose two of its three clinics.

Another cluster of laws aims to limit abortions based on possible reasons for having them, including sex selection and fetal diagnoses of conditions such as Down syndrome. Indiana's version, signed by then-Governor Mike Pence in 2016, was recently struck down by the United States Court of Appeals for the Seventh Circuit, 2-1.

As abortion court battles unfold, both sides say they will redouble their political efforts. Noting that the Senate this year did not pass a 20-week abortion ban, Mrs. Liebel of Susan B. Anthony's List said, "The focus for our political activity is to go door-to-door in seven states and flip some key Senate seats to be pro-life."

And Nancy Northup, president and chief executive of the Center for Reproductive Rights, which focuses on laws concerning reproductive freedom, noted that some eight states have enshrined the right to abortion, should Roe fall. "So we are also looking at advocacy alternatives, such as friendlier state laws and federal legislation to protect women's health," she said.

'I'm Doing It for the Babies': Inside the Ground Game to Reverse Roe v. Wade

BY ELIZABETH DIAS | JULY 20, 2018

AVON, IND. — Armed with sunscreen, doorknob fliers and a mission 50 years in the making, the team of activists sporting blue "I Vote Pro-Life" T-shirts fanned out into a web of cul-de-sacs in a subdivision just west of Indianapolis, undeterred by towering rain clouds and 90-degree heat.

It was exactly a week after President Trump had named Judge Brett M. Kavanaugh to be his nominee for the Supreme Court, and the group was joking that they had a new sport: Extreme Canvassing.

In short surveys, the teams ask voters about their hopes for Judge Kavanaugh's confirmation and their opposition to abortion funding. Canvassers have knocked at nearly 1.2 million homes nationwide in recent months, and by November, they are slated to reach their goal of 2 million.

"Whenever I'm feeling tired, I say, 'I'm doing it for the babies,' " said Kaiti Shannon, 19, as she consulted a mobile app to determine which porch with wind chimes to approach.

These are the ground troops of the social conservative movement, who have long dreamed of a nation where abortion is illegal. Ahead of the midterm elections, the Susan B. Anthony List, an anti-abortion political group, has dispatched hundreds of these canvassers across six battleground states. They aim to galvanize Americans who oppose abortion but who rarely vote outside presidential races, and to pressure red state Democrats, like Senator Joe Donnelly of Indiana, to support Judge Kavanaugh's confirmation.

Leaders of the anti-abortion movement believe they are closer than they have been in 50 years to achieving their goals, and local efforts like these are at the heart of their plan to get there. They see this political moment — a White House that advances anti-abortion priorities, a

Sandy Burton knocked on the door of a home in suburban Indiana while canvassing for the Susan B. Anthony List, an anti-abortion political group.

Supreme Court poised to tilt in a conservative direction, and a possible third Supreme Court seat to fill while Mr. Trump is still in office — as a rare opportunity, and one they have worked for years to create.

Some say they feel excited; others are cautiously optimistic. They are all definitely determined.

"Abortion is the single most significant human rights abuse of our time," said Jeanne Mancini, president of the March for Life, which has brought tens of thousands of protesters to Washington every year since the Supreme Court legalized abortion in 1973. "I have a lot of hope for incremental laws — for example, a late-term abortion ban."

While a majority of Americans have long believed abortion should be legal in most or all cases, the vocal anti-abortion movement is pursuing its goals at the local level. In states like Indiana, whose legislature has a Republican supermajority, activists have repeatedly pushed incremental laws that restrict abortion, require parental involvement or limit state funding.

Already, anti-abortion activists in Indiana hope that one of their laws, which gave a fetus nondiscrimination protections but was struck down in federal appeals court earlier this year, may be the one to challenge Roe v. Wade — if their attorney general appeals to the Supreme Court in the months ahead. But there are dozens of other cases working their way through the courts nationwide, including one involving an Iowa law banning almost all abortions after a fetal heartbeat is detected, and a Mississippi law banning abortion after 15 weeks. Seventeen states have laws that ban abortion after about 20 weeks.

These efforts reflect "a long-term and sophisticated strategy" to gain the upper hand, says Ilyse Hogue, president of the abortion rights organization Naral. "They've been stacking the courts, taking over state legislatures," she said in an interview, referring to anti-abortion groups. "This has been their plan. This is no doubt the day they have been waiting for."

As the canvassers dodged sprinklers in the Indiana suburbs, it was clear they saw their role as more than just a job for which they are paid $10 an hour: Many said they have opposed abortion most of their lives.

Joey Kurucz, 24, a law school student who has knocked on 2,600 Indiana doors, told the story of talking with voters in June when a dog bit his side, leaving a scar. He continued to shout questions at the owner from the safety of a neighbor's lawn. "They were pro-life!" he recalled with a smile.

Debra Minott, 62, said she spends 15 minutes every morning in silent prayer, asking for an end to abortion. She decided to go door-to-door five months ago, after regretting that she had not done more for the cause earlier in her life.

"I sometimes pick the worst days to go out, when it is so hot, because I want people to remember that I came to the door to advocate for life," Ms. Minott said, as she tucked a flier under a doormat.

California

Make appointment

No major
restrictions.

Get an abortion

Mississippi

Make appointment

Travel to only clinic

Asked to view ultrasound

State-directed counseling

Get parental consent

24-hour waiting period

Return to clinic

Pay out of pocket

Get an abortion

THE NEW YORK TIMES

Mississippi, which has only one abortion clinic, requires many more steps to undergo a procedure than California, which has 152 clinics and no major restrictions.

Their interactions with voters may be the linchpin of a calculated, top-down strategy, but on the streets, it feels more personal. At one house, a woman answered the door and shared her ambivalence about legalized abortion, recounting how she had one years ago. A canvasser asked if she could give her a hug.

A few streets away, a young man at first cracked his door just a few inches, holding it open with his toes to answer the survey. Eventually he stepped outside to say he does not want abortion to be used as birth control.

Another woman watching Fox News in her open garage said she wanted Judge Kavanaugh confirmed and Roe reversed, but that she also thought there were other ways to combat abortion, like promoting safe sex and using the morning after pill.

No one talked about the pending legal cases, and few discussed Mr. Trump. But their inherent opposition to abortion makes them prime candidates for national groups to organize.

The Susan B. Anthony List started its field program in force four years ago, and plans to spend at least $25 million on it ahead of this fall's midterm elections, up from $18 million in 2016. In some states, like Florida and West Virginia, their canvassers are also targeting persuadable voters, especially Hispanics, who oppose abortion at higher rates than white adults.

Other conservative evangelical and Catholic groups have been pouring money and resources into the battle to confirm Judge Kavanaugh this fall, which abortion rights groups pointed to as a vulnerability of the anti-abortion movement.

"The gains that have been made in the last few years have really come from a very small contingent of special-interest groups and powerful lobbyists," said Sara Hutchinson Ratcliffe, the vice president of Catholics for Choice, noting that a majority of Catholics believe abortion should be legal. "I don't think they have as many people in their corner as they think they do."

But as national attention focuses largely on the Supreme Court confirmation, movement leaders are hoping for political wins as well. In Minnesota, anti-abortion activists are zeroing in on the open governor's seat, considered a tossup. The Democratic governor, Mark Dayton, has vetoed seven bills supported by abortion opponents during his time in office.

"Our House and Senate are willing to pass this stuff," said Scott Fischbach, executive director of the Minnesota Citizens Concerned for Life, a group whose political arm helped push the State Legislature to an anti-abortion majority in recent years. "We are going to do more on this governor's race than we've ever done in the past."

Students for Life, a youth movement that calls itself "the pro-life generation," is starting a van tour in early August to six states — West Virginia, Indiana, North Dakota, Missouri, Alaska and Maine — to drum up support for Judge Kavanaugh's confirmation. Conservative statewide Christian groups, like the Ohio Christian Alliance, are urging thousands of local churches to have their members contact lawmakers to do the same.

Next month, the Susan B. Anthony List plans to host news conferences in front of the offices of vulnerable red-state Democrats, and to organize petitions and digital ad campaigns in an attempt to ramp up the political pressure to confirm Judge Kavanaugh.

For the activists on the ground in Indiana, there has already been a taste of victory: Former Gov. Mike Pence, champion of anti-abortion measures, is now in the White House.

"We knew that Indiana, our values, would be on the national stage," Mr. Kurucz, the canvasser who was bitten by the dog, said as he stepped up to another door. "I know we are pushing people to that successful result in November."

The Future of Abortion Under a New Supreme Court? Look to Arkansas

BY SABRINA TAVERNISE | SEPT. 7, 2018

FAYETTEVILLE, ARK. — When a patient arrived this spring at the only abortion clinic in western Arkansas, the doctor had startling news: A new state law had gone into effect, and clinics could no longer perform abortions via medication in the state.

"Wait — all of Arkansas?" the patient asked her doctor, Stephanie Ho.

"Yes," Dr. Ho remembered replying.

Less than a month later, a judge suspended the law, which is now the focus of a legal fight as Arkansas tries to reinstate it. In the meantime, Dr. Ho is working at one of the three remaining abortion clinics in the state, aware that, at any moment, she might have to stop performing abortions again.

The fight in Arkansas could help define the looming legal battle over abortion, 45 years after the Supreme Court made it a constitutional right. There are 14 abortion cases currently before federal appeals courts, including the Arkansas case, and legal experts say any of them could be the first to reach the Supreme Court after Justice Anthony Kennedy's retirement. Others include a parental consent law in Indiana, a ban on a common second-trimester abortion procedure in Alabama, and a requirement in Kentucky that ultrasounds be displayed and described.

The president's nomination of Brett M. Kavanaugh, a conservative federal judge, for the Supreme Court has added urgency to the question of whether Roe v. Wade will survive the Trump administration. In response to questions about abortion during his confirmation hearings this week, Judge Kavanaugh said he understood the significance of the issue and would respect the Supreme Court's "precedent on precedent."

But many legal experts say the more likely outcome of the change

Dr. Stephanie Ho had to cancel appointments with patients at Planned Parenthood Great Plains in Fayetteville, Ark., after the state put new regulations in place.

on the court, at least in the near term, will be less sweeping: States like Arkansas will get their way with smaller cases that reduce — but not eliminate — the right to an abortion.

"The Arkansas case is a bellwether, not because it's a frontal assault on Roe, but because it's another nudge in the direction of ever more restrictions on the right that Roe recognized," said Stephen I. Vladeck, a professor at the University of Texas School of Law in Austin. "It now becomes a much bigger story because we have this fundamental shift in the center of gravity."

Arkansas is in the heart of a broad band through the country's middle and south where abortion access in most states is already down to a few clinics. This map formed gradually, abortion rights advocates say, as red states passed laws that tested the boundaries of abortion restrictions, and federal appeals courts — in particular in the Eighth and Fifth Circuits — upheld them.

Federal appeals courts, the last stop before the Supreme Court, have the final say in most cases, because the Supreme Court takes very few.

Abortion opponents, who believe that the procedure destroys human life, argue that Roe is simply bad law. The Supreme Court stepped over the line in the ruling, they say, finding a constitutional right where there wasn't one and sweeping away established laws in dozens of states.

Abortion should be decided in state legislatures, said Steven Aden, general counsel of Americans United for Life. It would probably remain mostly legal in a third of the states, mostly illegal in another third, and be the subject of a furious fight in the rest, he said.

"That's the fight we think America should have," Mr. Aden said.

At least six states are down to one clinic — North Dakota, South Dakota, Wyoming, Kentucky, Mississippi and West Virginia. At times, Arkansas and Missouri had been a seventh and eighth.

The fight in Arkansas centers on medication abortions, which currently account for nearly a third of all abortions, according to the Guttmacher Institute. Medication abortions enable women up to 10 weeks pregnant to take two pills, the first supervised by a doctor and the second at home, to terminate a pregnancy without surgery. It was approved for use in 2000.

When the medication abortion law went into effect in Arkansas, it left only one clinic for a state of three million. That meant women from northwest Arkansas, where Dr. Ho practices, had to either go out of state or make a 380-mile round trip to Little Rock for a surgical abortion.

Now the number of clinics is back up to three. But many other barriers remain: a ban on abortions after 20 weeks; a 48-hour waiting period, which requires women to make two or three trips to the clinic; parental consent for minors; doctors unable to dispense medication abortion pills remotely by video.

"If you're a woman in Arkansas, and you're almost 200 miles away from a clinic, have a 48-hour waiting period, and a job that doesn't

Planned Parenthood runs two of Arkansas's three clinics. For decades, the state was controlled almost entirely by Democrats who largely backed abortion rights. That's changed during this decade.

give you sick leave or flexible hours, then your access to abortion has already been banned," said Helene Krasnoff, head of litigation at Planned Parenthood Federation of America. A regional branch of the organization, Planned Parenthood Great Plains, runs the clinic in Fayetteville, which provides medication abortion only.

The Arkansas law requires providers of medication abortion to have a written agreement with an obstetrician-gynecologist who has admitting privileges in a local hospital. Arkansas legislators who supported it said the law protects women's health by adding a layer of safety if something goes wrong.

The clinics said the procedure, which involves taking pills, is very safe, and sued. Meanwhile, all three abortion clinics tried to comply with the law. Dr. Ho testified in late June that letters were sent to all the obstetrician-gynecologists in the state with admitting privileges, asking for the required agreements. Planned Parenthood, which runs two of the clinics, including Dr. Ho's, said it sent more than 200 letters. None of the doctors agreed.

"You go through all these years of training, you hit all your milestones, and here comes somebody who knows nothing about what you do and says you are not competent," said Dr. Ho, a general practice doctor with training in performing abortions.

Abortion rights advocates argue that the law in Arkansas should not survive because the Supreme Court already weighed in when it struck down a similar law in Texas in 2016. The justices ruled that requiring hospital admitting privileges placed an undue burden on women seeking an abortion, violating their constitutional rights.

But because Arkansas is in the Eighth Circuit, with judges who tend to be more skeptical of abortion, the law stands a chance of being reinstated. Two other states, Missouri and Louisiana, also have laws similar to the Texas one in federal appeals courts now.

The lawyers for the Arkansas clinics asked the Supreme Court to hear the Arkansas case, but the justices declined without giving a reason.

A spokeswoman for Arkansas's attorney general, Leslie Rutledge, said in an email that Ms. Rutledge would "continue to do everything in her power to protect the health of Arkansas women" by fighting to reinstate the law. She pointed out that the Eighth Circuit "had unanimously ruled" that a judge's move to block the law "was incorrect," and the fact that the Supreme Court did not take the case shows that the justices did not believe the clinics' argument.

Legal experts said it was impossible to know the Supreme Court's reasoning or whether the justices would agree to take the case if they were asked again.

The large number of abortion restrictions is relatively new for Arkansas. For decades, the state was run almost entirely by Democrats who largely backed abortion rights. As recently as 2011, Democrats held five of the state's six offices in Washington, controlled all of its statewide offices, including the governor's mansion, and had majorities in both chambers of its legislature, said Jay Barth, a politics professor at Hendrix College in Conway, Ark. It was the last state in the South to come under Republican control, he said.

But in 2012, Democrats lost control of both houses — the first time since 1874, according to Professor Barth — and by 2015, there was not a single Arkansas Democrat in elected office in Washington or at the statewide level in Little Rock.

The state has passed 29 laws restricting abortion since 2011, the third most in the country after Kansas and Indiana, said Elizabeth Nash, a senior policy analyst for the Guttmacher Institute. Across the country, state legislatures have passed 423 abortion restrictions since Republicans swept statehouses in 2010, Ms. Nash said. That is about 35 percent of all abortion legislation that has passed since 1973.

Some of these laws wound up in court, where they have increasingly received a more sympathetic hearing as some federal appeals courts have grown more conservative.

"The noose is tightening," said Bettina E. Brownstein, a lawyer in Little Rock who represents abortion clinics. "The courts are not the avenue they once were. That's the big difference."

Today, Republican presidents have appointed 10 of the 11 judges on the Eighth Circuit, compared to six in 2001, according to Russell Wheeler, a visiting fellow at the Brookings Institution in Washington.

While Arkansas politics were shifting, Dr. Ho was finishing her residency program at the University of Arkansas. She had decided early in her career that she was going to provide abortion care, but it was not an easy choice.

She remembers a doctor in her residency program asking, in exasperation: "Why do you even want to do this?" She replied: "If I can and I'm willing, why would I not?"

Dr. Ho said she had to pay her own way and go out of state to Colorado to get a month of abortion training. After she finished residency, she interviewed for jobs but no one offered her one. She said one interviewer told her directly that her intention to provide abortions meant she would not be invited back.

For now, she is continuing her work, but that could change anytime. The stakes are high: A ruling against the clinics would effectively ban medication abortion in the state and leave Arkansas again with only one clinic. But a ruling against the state, Professor Vladeck believes, could mean the case ends up at the Supreme Court, potentially setting a new legal standard for lower courts that clinics might find worse.

"It's going to be a very different Supreme Court going forward," Professor Vladeck said.

The Handmaid's Court

OPINION | BY MICHELLE GOLDBERG | SEPT. 10, 2018

SHORTLY AFTER HIS INAUGURATION, Donald Trump, uniquely attentive to his debt to the religious right, appointed the anti-abortion activist E. Scott Lloyd to head the Office of Refugee Resettlement, despite Lloyd's lack of relevant experience. The position gave Lloyd authority over unaccompanied minors caught crossing into the United States, authority Lloyd exploited to try to stop pregnant migrants from getting abortions.

Last year, thanks to Lloyd's interference, a 17-year-old from Central America had to wage a legal battle to end her pregnancy. Known in court filings as Jane Doe, the girl learned she was pregnant while in custody in Texas, and was adamant that she wanted an abortion. In keeping with Texas's parental consent law, she obtained a judge's permission, helped by a legal organization called Jane's Due Process. Jane's Due Process raised money for the abortion, which was scheduled for the end of her first trimester.

But under Lloyd's direction, the shelter where she was being detained refused to cooperate. Doe went back to court, and a federal judge ruled in her favor, issuing a temporary restraining order against the government. The administration appealed, and the case, Garza v. Hargan, went to a three-judge panel of the Court of Appeals for the District of Columbia Circuit. One of the judges was Brett Kavanaugh.

Garza v. Hargan was the only major abortion-rights case Kavanaugh ever ruled on. His handling of it offers a clue about what's in store for American women if he's confirmed to the Supreme Court. No one knows whether Kavanaugh would vote to overturn Roe v. Wade outright or simply gut it. But even on a lower court, Kavanaugh put arbitrary obstacles in the way of someone desperate to end her pregnancy. Thanks to Trump, he may soon be in a position to do the same to millions of others.

A protester dressed as a character from "The Handmaid's Tale" attended the first day of Brett Kavanaugh's confirmation hearing last week.

It's fitting that last week's Kavanaugh confirmation hearings were regularly interrupted by the sound of women screaming. Again and again, protesters, most of them female, cried out for the preservation of their rights, and were arrested. Republican men were contemptuous. "What's the hysteria coming from?" asked Senator Ben Sasse of Nebraska.

Let me answer. It is true, as Sasse said, that protesters have claimed for many years that if Roe v. Wade is overturned, women will die. It's a fair prediction; women died before Roe, and where abortion is illegal, unsafe abortion leads to maternal death. In the past, however, Roe has been saved. Should Kavanaugh be confirmed, it will either fall or be eviscerated.

In Garza, Kavanaugh and another judge vacated the temporary restraining order that prevented the government from hindering Doe's abortion. Brigitte Amiri, an A.C.L.U. lawyer who represented the girl, was stunned, because it seemed clear that Doe, who'd already obtained the necessary judicial signoff, had the law on her side. "It wasn't what I was expecting from any judge that would have read Roe v. Wade," Amiri said of the ruling. "Conservatives, progressives, anyone."

Indeed, a few days later, the full court reversed the panel's decision. Kavanaugh, dissenting, wrote that "the government has permissible interests in favoring fetal life."

By the time Jane Doe got her abortion, she was 15 weeks pregnant and needed a more complicated second-trimester procedure. On Friday, Rochelle Garza, a lawyer who served as Doe's temporary legal guardian during the proceedings, testified at Kavanaugh's confirmation hearings.

"She was one of the most vulnerable people in our community," Garza said of the girl, adding, "She was an immigrant, she didn't speak English, she was in detention, and she was being put under extreme pressure. And I felt it was unfortunate that Judge Kavanaugh did not take that into consideration."

We shouldn't expect a Trump nominee, however personally decent his friends say he is, to care about women's wishes. Kavanaugh's defenders insist that he's the sort of judge any Republican would appoint, and they are correct. Still, it's a particularly bitter insult that women stand to lose reproductive autonomy thanks to the minority presidential victory of a louche misogynist.

Politicians sometimes say that they are personally opposed to abortion, but believe it should be legal. Trump and some of his enablers reverse that formulation.

The president, who does not, according to two of his lovers, wear condoms, has declined to say whether he's ever been involved with an abortion. According to court papers unsealed on Friday, Elliott Broidy, former deputy finance chairman of the Republican National Committee, also refused to wear condoms during sex with his mistress, Shera Bechard, then demanded she get an abortion when she became pregnant. According to the unsealed papers, Broidy admired

Trump's "uncanny ability to sexually abuse woman and get away with it."

A famous pro-choice poster from the 1980s proclaimed, "Your body is a battleground." Kavanaugh is likely to join the Supreme Court because in 2016, the woman whom most women voted for was defeated. Now our bodies are subject to occupation.

MICHELLE GOLDBERG has been an Opinion columnist since 2017. She is the author of several books about politics, religion and women's rights, and was part of a team that won a Pulitzer Prize for public service in 2018 for reporting on workplace sexual harassment issues.

Why I Wanted to Learn to Perform Abortions

BY JEN GUNTER | OCT. 14, 2018

With the future of contraception in question, looking back to recent history is instructive.

IT STARTS WITH STEEL.

A speculum. A needle. A tenaculum to steady the cervix. A set of dilators. These were the instruments I used when I trained to perform abortions in the 1990s.

There was also plastic and suction. The equipment was all so hard and sharp, and yet the procedure itself required a delicate touch. This was before ultrasound was commonly used, so a surgical abortion was often performed blindly. It took experience to recognize and understand the feel of steel and hard plastic on the cervix and the uterus. Not just because you couldn't see, but also because the tissue changes week by week as the uterus enlarges and the muscle thins.

As the pregnancy advances there are also fetal bones, which are sharp and can lacerate the uterus, blood vessels or bowel. The result can be maternal death if a surgeon doesn't intervene quickly.

All of this probably sounds dangerous, but in skilled hands and with appropriate equipment a surgical abortion is one of the safest medical procedures any person can undergo.

Though we often think of abortion as a choice, some come out of medical necessity. For example, in the case of an intrauterine pre-viability infection (that's around 24 weeks), the recommendation is delivery or the infection can be lethal.

In this situation some women choose a surgical abortion, while others prefer to labor. It's really hard to call it a preference. But the options offer some measure of control for the pregnant person, and controlling even one thing can be comforting when everything else, medically speaking, seems out of control.

These personal and medical decisions are difficult enough. Now the specter of legislation is creeping into doctors' offices and labor and delivery suites. Conversations we should never entertain — ones that start with, "Is she sick enough yet?" — are becoming more common.

Imagine if your well-trained pilot were expertly managing a sudden loss of altitude mid-flight but had to step away to consult a lawyer to figure out if a reasonable pilot would conclude a crash was imminent, only to find that imminent isn't even defined?

This idea of pleading abortion worthiness was the very thing that drove me into obstetrics and gynecology. When I was in high school in Canada, a woman wanting an abortion had to present her case to an "abortion panel," a three-person tribunal (pretty medieval, no?). Women would confide their circumstances to their own doctor, who would hopefully send a report to a panel of three unknown doctors.

If their stories were to be sympathetic, these women had to adhere to certain guiding principles: Be contrite. Apologize. Promise to do better. Smile, but in a sad way. Don't say too much, but say enough. Walk the edge of the knife between self-pity and responsibility. And hope they don't know your parents.

We coached our friends the best we could, but I was determined to do better.

So during my obstetrics and gynecology residency I spent much of my free time learning abortions. The training was available to all, but not embedded in the program, so I had to go out of my way to learn. I can think of no other surgical specialty where a procedure is so common that 24 percent of patients will have one by the age of 45 and yet it has been deemed "elective" to learn.

I was trained to do abortions by men who, interestingly enough, had financial and social backgrounds similar to those of many men who currently write and interpret our abortion laws. What makes one man weep remembering a young nurse dying from a pelvic abscess incurred in a clandestine abortion, and another man want to erase her with legislation?

We had a few female OB-GYNs in my training program, probably similar to most training programs in the 1990s, but it was men who taught me how to perform abortions. At the time I thought it odd. In retrospect, I wonder if women steered clear because abortion could be one more thing held against them. No other surgical procedure is weaponized so effectively, and in so many ways, against women.

Along with the skill to do abortions, the men who taught me also passed on their experience from when abortion was illegal. (It was legalized in the U.S. in 1973 and in Canada in 1969.) They taught me about catastrophic infections. Spilled bowel contents from instruments that had lacerated the uterus and large intestine. Family members who hung up on calls from their facilities because they preferred not to know what was going on with their daughters. They told me of women dying alone.

They never said where these women had met their fate. A well-meaning but ill-trained doctor or friend? A true medical profiteer taking advantage of a woman's predicament?

Once upon a time some doctors could get away with offering early abortions by calling them "menstrual extractions," which were meant to remove built-up uterine lining supposedly caused by a hormonal imbalance. Accurate pregnancy tests were not available until the 1970s, and so a missed period or two could plausibly be explained this way. But not so often as to arouse legal suspicion.

The whisper network may have sent some women with money to these well-trained providers with clean equipment, but it sent others to unskilled hands with rusted equipment. Women would choose this man in that neighborhood over another man in another neighborhood because they had heard maybe he was not as bad, his facility was a little cleaner.

Sometimes they would go in knowing he was the worst but hoped for the best because he was all they could afford.

Some women take time to reach their decision and others know immediately. But once they know, they know.

Indecision doesn't lead a woman to put her feet in stirrups, lay back and hope the person holding the steel is well-trained and trustworthy. No one who is unsure of a medical decision would consider a filthy man with filthy equipment in a filthy room a viable option.

Even though women know their bodies and their minds, many states require doctors to explain pregnancy to a woman, as if she were an impulsive child. No woman in the history of women has ever said, "Oh doctor, thank you so much for explaining. I didn't realize what pregnancy meant."

These and other regulations are not about patient safety or informed consent. They are intended to make the procedure more expensive or harder to access.

If men are going to regulate the uterus, they should have the courage to be honest about their decisions and motivations. Restrictive and deterring abortion laws do not help make the practice of abortion safer. In the end, they force women to choose poverty or a fetal skull perforating the uterus. It would take a lot less courage for legislators to admit their intentions than it does for a woman to entrust her body to an unnamed man in a dirty room.

DR. JEN GUNTER is an obstetrician and gynecologist practicing in California. The Cycle, a column on women's reproductive health, appears regularly in Styles.

Glossary

&c. Alternative form of "etc"; short for "et cetera," which is Latin for "and so forth."

abortifacient A substance that terminates a pregnancy.

abortion The intentional termination of a pregnancy.

advocate To publicly support or argue for a cause; a person who publicly supports or argues for a cause.

birth control The prevention of unwanted pregnancies.

conception The act of conceiving a child.

embryo Unborn offspring in an early stage of development.

fertilization The process by which male sperm fuses with a female egg to create a zygote, which will develop into a baby.

fetus Unborn offspring in the prenatal stage that occurs between the embryonic stage and birth.

gynecologist A doctor that specializes in dealing with the functions and diseases of women's reproductive organs.

implantation The moment when a fertilized egg implants into a woman's uterus; this is a necessary step in conception.

intrauterine device (IUD) A device that is implanted in a woman's uterus to prevent a fertilized egg from implanting; a contraceptive device.

legal precedent A legal case that establishes a guiding principle or rule.

miscarriage An event that results in a pregnancy ending on its own.

morning-after pill An emergency birth control pill that women can take up to seventy-two hours after unprotected sex to prevent pregnancy. Depending on the pill and the time during which it is taken, it can prevent ovulation, fertilization or implantation.

partial-birth abortion An abortion occurring in a late stage of pregnancy in which the fetus has already died or is killed before removal.

Planned Parenthood A nonprofit organization providing sexual and reproductive health care, including abortion.

pro-choice The ideological stance that a woman should have the legal right to seek out an abortion.

pro-life The ideological stance that abortion is wrong and should be illegal.

stem cell A type of biological cell that has the capability of developing into other types of cells.

sterilization Any procedure or process that results in a man or woman being unable to reproduce.

Media Literacy Terms

"Media literacy" refers to the ability to access, understand, critically assess and create media. The following terms are important components of media literacy, and they will help you critically engage with the articles in this title.

angle The aspect of a news story on which a journalist focuses and develops.

attribution The method by which a source is identified or by which facts and information are assigned to the person who provided them.

balance Principle of journalism that both perspectives of an argument should be presented in a fair way.

chronological order Method of writing a story presenting the details of the story in the order in which they occurred.

commentary Type of story that is an expression of opinion on recent events by a journalist generally known as a commentator.

credibility The quality of being trustworthy and believable, said of a journalistic source.

critical review Type of story that describes an event or work of art, such as a theater performance, film, concert, book, restaurant, radio or television program, exhibition or musical piece, and offers critical assessment of its quality and reception.

editorial Article of opinion or interpretation.

feature story Article designed to entertain as well as to inform.

headline Type, usually 18 point or larger, used to introduce a story.

human interest story Type of story that focuses on individuals and how events or issues affect their lives, generally offering a sense of relatability to the reader.

impartiality Principle of journalism that a story should not reflect a journalist's bias and should contain balance.

intention The motive or reason behind something, such as the publication of a news story.

interview story Type of story in which the facts are gathered primarily by interviewing another person or persons.

motive The reason behind something, such as the publication of a news story or a source's perspective on an issue.

news story An article or style of expository writing that reports news, generally in a straightforward fashion and without editorial comment.

op-ed An opinion piece that reflects a prominent individual's opinion on a topic of interest.

paraphrase The summary of an individual's words, with attribution, rather than a direct quotation of their exact words.

plagiarism An attempt to pass another person's work as one's own without attribution.

quotation The use of an individual's exact words indicated by the use of quotation marks and proper attribution.

reliability The quality of being dependable and accurate, said of a journalistic source.

rhetorical device Technique in writing intending to persuade the reader or communicate a message from a certain perspective.

source The origin of the information reported in journalism.

tone A manner of expression in writing or speech.

Media Literacy Questions

1. "As Congressmen Take Up the Abortion Issue, Two Sides Debate: When Does Life Begin?" (on page 57) is an example of an interview. What are the benefits of providing readers with direct quotes of an interviewed subject's speech? Is the subject of an interview always a reliable source?

2. "Who Can Choose?" (on page 153) is an example of a critical review. What is the purpose of a critical review? Do you feel this article achieved that purpose?

3. The article "The Handmaid's Court" (on page 203) is an example of an op-ed. Identify how Michelle Goldberg's attitude and tone help convey her opinion on the topic.

4. What is the intention of the article "The Supreme Court as Moral Arbiter" (on page 54)? How effectively does it achieve its intended purpose?

5. Does Sheryl Gay Stolberg demonstrate the journalistic principle of balance in her article "In Support of Abortion, It's Personal vs. Political" (on page 104)? If so, how did she do so? If not, what could she have included to make the article more balanced?

6. "The Future of Abortion Under a New Supreme Court? Look to Arkansas" (on page 196) features photographs. What do the photographs add to the article?

7. Identify the various sources cited in the article "After Stem-Cell Rift, Groups Unite for Anti-Abortion Push" (on page 146). How do the journalists attribute information to each of these sources in their article? How effective are their attributions in helping the reader identify their sources?

8. Compare the headlines of "Drive Against Abortion Finds a Symbol: Wichita" (on page 120) and "Face of Protests in Wichita Is Religious and Undoubting" (on page 124). Which is a more compelling headline, and why? How could the less compelling headline be changed to better draw the reader's interest?

9. Identify each of the sources in "Legal Abortion Under Fierce Attack 15 Years After Roe v. Wade Ruling" (on page 67) as a primary source or a secondary source. Evaluate the reliability and credibility of each source. How does your evaluation of each source change your perspective on this article?

10. Analyze the journalists' reporting in "Opponents of Abortions Cheer New Administration" (on page 94) and "Bush Rule Makes Fetuses Eligible for Health Benefits" (on page 98). Do you think one journalist is more impartial in their reporting than the other? If so, why do you think so?

Citations

All citations in this list are formatted according to the
Modern Language Association's (MLA) style guide.

BOOK CITATION

THE NEW YORK TIMES EDITORIAL STAFF. *Abortion*. New York: New York Times
Educational Publishing, 2019.

ONLINE ARTICLE CITATIONS

BARRINGER, FELICITY. "Abortion Clinics Preparing for More Violence." *The
New York Times*, 12 Mar. 1993, https://www.nytimes.com/1993/03/12/us
/abortion-clinics-preparing-for-more-violence.html.

BELLUCK, PAM, AND JAN HOFFMAN. "Bulwark Against an Abortion Ban? Medical Advances." *The New York Times*, 1 July 2018, https://www.nytimes
.com/2018/07/01/science/abortion-supreme-court-trump.html.

BRODY, JANE E. "Abortion: Once a Whispered Problem, Now a Public Debate."
The New York Times, 8 Jan. 1968, https://timesmachine.nytimes.com
/timesmachine/1968/01/08/91219771.pdf.

CALMES, JACKIE. "Advocates Shun 'Pro-Choice' to Expand Message." *The New
York Times*, 28 July 2014, https://www.nytimes.com/2014/07/29/us/politics
/advocates-shun-pro-choice-to-expand-message.html.

CLARITY, JAMES F. "Again the Abortion Issue." *The New York Times*, 14 Jan. 1968,
https://timesmachine.nytimes.com/timesmachine/1968/01/14/89315513.pdf.

DEGNAN, DANIEL A. "The Supreme Court as Moral Arbiter." *The New York
Times*, 10 Mar. 1973, https://www.nytimes.com/1973/03/10/archives
/the-supreme-court-as-moral-arbiter.html.

DEMASTERS, KAREN. "Planned Parenthood Will Offer Early Abortion Procedures." *The New York Times*, 28 Dec. 1997, https://www.nytimes.com
/1997/12/28/nyregion/in-brief-planned-parenthood-will-offer-early
-abortion-procedures.html.

DIAS, ELIZABETH. " 'I'm Doing It for the Babies': Inside the Ground Game to Reverse Roe v. Wade." *The New York Times*, 20 July 2018, https://www.nytimes.com/2018/07/20/us/politics/anti-abortion-roe-v-wade.html.

DIONNE, E. J., JR. "Abortion Rights Backers Adopt Tactics of Politics." *The New York Times*, 21 July 1989, https://www.nytimes.com/1989/07/21/us/abortion-rights-backers-adopt-tactics-of-politics.html.

DIONNE, E. J., JR. "Foes of Abortion Prepare Measures for State Action." *The New York Times*, 5 July 1989, https://www.nytimes.com/1989/07/05/us/foes-of-abortion-prepare-measures-for-state-action.html.

ELLIOTT, STUART. "Pro Bono TV Spot for Abortion Rights." *The New York Times*, 1 Mar. 1994, https://www.nytimes.com/1994/03/01/business/the-media-business-advertising-addenda-pro-bono-tv-spot-for-abortion-rights.html.

GOLDBERG, MICHELLE. "The Handmaid's Court." *The New York Times*, 10 Sept. 2018, https://www.nytimes.com/2018/09/10/opinion/columnists/kavanaugh-abortion-roe-v-wade-trump.html.

GREENHOUSE, LINDA. "High Court, 5-4, Affirms Right to Abortion But Allows Most of Pennsylvania's Limits." *The New York Times*, 30 June 1992, https://www.nytimes.com/1992/06/30/us/supreme-court-high-court-5-4-affirms-right-abortion-but-allows-most-pennsylvania.html.

GUNTER, JEN. "Why I Wanted to Learn to Perform Abortions." *The New York Times*, 14 Oct. 2018, https://www.nytimes.com/2018/10/14/style/performing-abortions.html.

KAPLAN, MORRIS. "Abortion and Sterilization Win Support of Planned Parenthood." *The New York Times*, 14 Nov. 1968, https://timesmachine.nytimes.com/timesmachine/1968/11/14/76906773.pdf.

KIFNER, JOHN. "Religious Searching Leads to the Anti-Abortion Movement." *The New York Times*, 30 Mar. 2001, https://www.nytimes.com/2001/03/30/nyregion/religious-searching-leads-to-the-anti-abortion-movement.html.

LEWIN, TAMAR. "Anthrax Scare Hits Groups Backing Right to Abortion." *The New York Times*, 9 Nov. 2001, https://www.nytimes.com/2001/11/09/us/anthrax-scare-hits-groups-backing-right-to-abortion.html.

LEWIN, TAMAR. "Legal Abortion Under Fierce Attack 15 Years After Roe v. Wade Ruling." *The New York Times*, 10 May 1988, https://www.nytimes.com/1988/05/10/us/legal-abortion-under-fierce-attack-15-years-after-roe-v-wade-ruling.html.

LEWIS, ANTHONY. "Legal Abortions Proposed in Code." *The New York Times*,

22 May 1959, https://timesmachine.nytimes.com/timesmachine/1959
/05/22/89200531.pdf.

LIPTAK, ADAM. "Ruling Opens New Arena in the Debate on Abortion." *The New York Times*, 16 Oct. 2002, https://www.nytimes.com/2002/10/16/us /ruling-opens-new-arena-in-the-debate-on-abortion.html.

LIPTAK, ADAM. "Supreme Court Backs Anti-Abortion Pregnancy Centers in Free Speech Case." *The New York Times*, 26 June 2018, https://www .nytimes.com/2018/06/26/us/politics/supreme-court-crisis-pregnancy -center-abortion.html.

LUCERO, LOUIS, II. "Walgreens Pharmacist Denies Woman With Unviable Pregnancy the Medication Needed to End It." *The New York Times*, 25 June 2018, https://www.nytimes.com/2018/06/25/us/walgreens-pharmacist -pregnancy-miscarriage.html.

MANSNERUS, LAURA. "What Is Right and Wrong With Roe v. Wade?" *The New York Times*, 23 Apr. 1989, https://www.nytimes.com/1989/04/23 /weekinreview/nation-what-right-wrong-with-roe-v-wade-view -friends-court.html.

THE NEW YORK TIMES. "Abortion Suit Is Filed." *The New York Times*, 26 July 1962, https://timesmachine.nytimes.com/timesmachine/1962 /07/26/80436097.pdf.

THE NEW YORK TIMES. "As Congressmen Take Up the Abortion Issue, Two Sides Debate: When Does Life Begin?" *The New York Times*, 19 Apr. 1981, https://www.nytimes.com/1981/04/19/weekinreview/as-congressmen-take -up-the-abortion-issue-two-sides-debate-when-does-life-begin.html.

THE NEW YORK TIMES. "Contempt for Abortion, and Tolerance." *The New York Times*, 27 Jan. 1986, https://www.nytimes.com/1986/01/27/opinion /contempt-for-abortion-and-tolerance.html.

THE NEW YORK TIMES. "Dilemma Is Seen in Abortion Law." *The New York Times*, 28 July 1959, https://timesmachine.nytimes.com/timesmachine /1959/07/28/80540680.pdf.

THE NEW YORK TIMES. "Doctors and Nurses Held." *The New York Times*, 12 July 1937, https://timesmachine.nytimes.com/timesmachine/1937 /07/12/94399145.pdf.

THE NEW YORK TIMES. "Examinations in the Malpractice Cases." *The New York Times*, 24 Apr. 1873, https://timesmachine.nytimes.com/timesmachine /1873/04/24/82406227.pdf.

THE NEW YORK TIMES. "Excerpts From Abortion Case." *The New York Times*,

23 Jan. 1973, https://www.nytimes.com/1973/01/23/archives/excerpts-from
-abortion-case-privacy-rights-unclear.html.

THE NEW YORK TIMES. "Illegal Operations Laid to 3 Doctors." *The New York Times*, 16 Nov. 1940, https://timesmachine.nytimes.com/timesmachine
/1940/11/16/94013057.pdf.

THE NEW YORK TIMES. "Mrs. Finkbine Undergoes Abortion in Sweden."
The New York Times, 19 Aug. 1962, https://timesmachine.nytimes.com
/timesmachine/1962/08/19/90573225.pdf.

THE NEW YORK TIMES. " ' Partial Birth' Deceptions." *The New York Times*, 20 Oct. 1999, https://www.nytimes.com/1999/10/20/opinion/partial-birth
-deceptions.html.

THE NEW YORK TIMES. "The Partial-Birth Stratagem." *The New York Times*, 16 May 1998, https://www.nytimes.com/1998/05/16/opinion/the-partial
-birth-stratagem.html.

THE NEW YORK TIMES. "Phoenix Abortion Ruling Delayed." *The New York Times*, 28 July 1962, https://timesmachine.nytimes.com/timesmachine
/1962/07/28/87314786.pdf.

THE NEW YORK TIMES. "Posturing on Abortion." *The New York Times*, 19 Apr. 2002, https://www.nytimes.com/2002/04/19/opinion/posturing-on-abortion.html.

THE NEW YORK TIMES. "Ruling Allows Major Center Its First Clinic for Abortions." *The New York Times*, 15 Feb. 1998, https://www.nytimes.com/1998/02/15/us
/ruling-allows-major-center-its-first-clinic-for-abortions.html.

THE NEW YORK TIMES. "Suggests Doctors Relax 'Hypocrisy.' " *The New York Times*, 31 Jan. 1942, https://timesmachine.nytimes.com/timesmachine
/1942/01/31/85513277.pdf.

THE NEW YORK TIMES. "Woman Juror Fails to End a Deadlock." *The New York Times*, 7 Oct. 1937, https://timesmachine.nytimes.com/timesmachine/1937
/10/07/94435540.pdf.

PEAR, ROBERT. "Bush Rule Makes Fetuses Eligible for Health Benefits." *The New York Times*, 28 Sept. 2002, https://www.nytimes.com/2002/09/28/us
/bush-rule-makes-fetuses-eligible-for-health-benefits.html.

PRESS, EYAL. "Who Can Choose?" *The New York Times*, 3 Feb. 2002, https://
www.nytimes.com/2002/02/03/books/who-can-choose.html.

SACK, KEVIN, AND GUSTAV NIEBUHR. "After Stem-Cell Rift, Groups Unite
for Anti-Abortion Push." *The New York Times*, 4 Sept. 2001, https://www
.nytimes.com/2001/09/04/us/after-stem-cell-rift-groups-unite-for-anti
-abortion-push.html.

SHRAGE, LAURIE. "How to Talk About Abortion." *The New York Times*, 19 Mar. 2018, https://www.nytimes.com/2018/03/19/opinion/abortion-arguments-morality-policy.html.

STOLBERG, SHERYL GAY. "In Support of Abortion, It's Personal vs. Political." *The New York Times*, 28 Nov. 2009, https://www.nytimes.com/2009/11/29/weekinreview/29stolberg.html.

STOLBERG, SHERYL GAY. "Legal Fight Could Make Kentucky Only State With No Abortion Clinic." *The New York Times*, 2 May 2017, https://www.nytimes.com/2017/05/02/us/kentucky-abortion-clinic.html.

TAVERNISE, SABRINA. "The Future of Abortion Under a New Supreme Court? Look to Arkansas." *The New York Times*, 7 Sept. 2018, https://www.nytimes.com/2018/09/07/us/abortion-supreme-court-arkansas.html.

TERRY, DON. "Face of Protests in Wichita Is Religious and Undoubting." *The New York Times*, 12 Aug. 1991, https://www.nytimes.com/1991/08/12/us/face-of-protests-in-wichita-is-religious-and-undoubting.html.

TONER, ROBIN. "Opponents of Abortions Cheer New Administration." *The New York Times*, 23 Jan. 2001, https://www.nytimes.com/2001/01/23/us/new-administration-abortion-issue-opponents-abortions-cheer-new-administration.html.

VERHOVEK, SAM HOWE. "Anti-Abortion Site on Web Has Ignited Free Speech Debate." *The New York Times*, 13 Jan. 1999, https://www.nytimes.com/1999/01/13/us/anti-abortion-site-on-web-has-ignited-free-speech-debate.html.

WEAVER, WARREN, JR. "National Guidelines Set by 7-to-2 Vote." *The New York Times*, 23 Jan. 1973, https://www.nytimes.com/1973/01/23/archives/national-guidelines-set-by-7to2-vote-high-court-backs-abortions-in.html.

WILKERSON, ISABEL. "Drive Against Abortion Finds a Symbol: Wichita." *The New York Times*, 4 Aug. 1991, https://www.nytimes.com/1991/08/04/us/drive-against-abortion-finds-a-symbol-wichita.html.

ZIEGLER, MARY. "Roe v. Wade Was About More Than Abortion." *The New York Times*, 21 Jan. 2018, https://www.nytimes.com/2018/01/21/opinion/roe-v-wade-abortion.html.

ZIEGLER, MARY. "Where the Pro-Life Movement Goes Next." *The New York Times*, 2 July 2016, https://www.nytimes.com/2016/07/03/opinion/sunday/where-the-pro-life-movement-goes-next.html.

Index

This book is current up until the time of printing. For the most up-to-date reporting, visit www.nytimes.com.